Win Wenger's
IMAGE-STREAMING

by
Charles Roman

Project Renaissance
Gaithersburg, MD
2006

ISBN 978-1-4303-1862-0

© 2006 Win Wenger and Charles P. Roman

All rights reserved. No part of this book may be reproduced or transmitted in any form or by any means, electronic or mechanical, including photocopying, recording, or by any information storage or retrieval system, without written permission from Win Wenger or Charles Roman, except for the inclusion of brief quotations in a review.

Cover design:
Kate Jones

Original illustrations:
Jamie Murphy

Cover photography:
Elan Sun Star

Acknowledgments

The contents of this book are based upon the life's work of Win Wenger, Ph.D., the founder of Project Renaissance. Since the early 1970's, Dr. Wenger has been developing and making available to all of us a variety of valuable processes and techniques through his non-profit educational organizations. The author thanks Dr. Wenger for the opportunity to work on this book.

Sincere thanks also go to Kate Jones, chief editor for this series of Core Books, for her continuing work in support of Project Renaissance and for the design of this book.

— *Charles Roman*

"Keep on going and the chances are you will stumble on something, perhaps when you are least expecting it. I have never heard of anyone stumbling on something sitting down."
— *Charles Kettering*

"From Image-Streaming on down — Win Wenger has been and is a massively influential character in the world of personal and professional development. His work, usually unattributed, has influenced the whole field of personal development. He's cool!"
— *Michael Breen*

"Dr. Win Wenger's 30 years of study show that genius is not a result of genetic superiority, but of a pattern of mental conditioning. Which means, genius is within your grasp."
— *Learning Strategies*

About the Author

Charles Roman has a BS in Physics from Carnegie-Mellon University and an MS in Nuclear Engineering from Rensselaer Polytechnic Institute. He lives in Pittsburgh, PA, where he is a project manager for Westinghouse Electric Co., LLC, and a former certified senior reactor operator instructor.

Chuck first met Win Wenger at Project Renaissance's annual Double Festival in 2002. Since then, he has continued to study and practice the techniques of Project Renaissance and has expanded into other areas of interest. He teaches classes in creative problem-solving and accelerated learning. He is a certified trainer on behalf of Project Renaissance.

About Win Wenger

Win Wenger, Ph.D., is a pioneer in the fields of creativity and creative method, accelerated learning, brain and mind development, and political economy.

Formerly a college teacher, Dr. Wenger is a trainer renowned around the world, and the author of 48 published books, including his breakthrough text of techniques to facilitate scientific discovery and technical invention, *Discovering the Obvious*.

His main text of education-related and growth techniques is *Beyond Teaching and Learning*, and his most widely popular work, *The Einstein Factor*, co-authored with Richard Poe, is available in good bookstores near you. Another great work by Win is *How to Increase Your Intelligence*. Synopses of his work, and special articles on it, have frequently appeared in *Success* Magazine, one of the world's leading entrepreneurial monthlies.

Table of Contents

Preface iii
Acknowledgments v
About the Author vii
About Win Wenger vii
Introduction 3
    A Guaranteed Way to Improve Your Intelligence 4
    Image-Streaming: How It Builds Intelligence 6
Chapter 1: You Are Brighter Than You Think 10
    Image-Streaming: The Process 10
    "Co-Tripping" with a Partner 14
    Insomniac's Special 14
    The Creativity Break 15
    Writer's Block – Fiction 16
    Writer's Block – Non-Fiction 17
    Prompting Techniques 19
    Sensory Attributes 22
    Building and Enhancing Your Image-Stream 25
    Record and Learn from Your Experiences 28
Chapter 2: Creative Problem-Solving 29
    Image-Streaming for Creative Problem-Solving 30
    Validation 34
    Over the Wall 35
    Short Form of Over the Wall 41
    Getting the Meaning from Your Images 42
    Follow-up Questions 44
    Other Triggers 45

Finding Problems 46
Dreams 49
Chapter 3: Accelerated Learning 51
Instant Replay 52
Predictive Imagery 56
What Did I Leave Out? 58
Cognitive Structural Enhancement 59
Chapter 4: Image-Streaming for Children 64
Help a Young Child to Flower 64
Practical Problem-Solving for Children 66
The World Next Door 67
Chapter 5: Image-Streaming for Groups 73
Chapter 6: High Thinktank 79
Bypassing Our Internal Editor 79
Truly Great Problems 80
Group High Thinktank 81
High Thinktank When Working Alone 83
The 30-day Challenge 84
Closing Remarks 89
Appendix A 90
Appendix B 92
Appendix C 94
Appendix D 103
Appendix E 105

IMAGE-STREAMING

Introduction

Have you ever had a solution to a problem that you weren't consciously thinking about come to you suddenly (an "Aha!" experience)?

Have you ever done something as a result of a *hunch* and have it turn out right on target?

Have you ever driven home from work and wondered how you got there? You can't remember whether that last traffic light was red or green as you approached it!

If you have ever had one of these experiences, did you ever wonder how these things happened? Apparently, there is much more activity occurring within our minds than we consciously recognize. These incidents, along with other evidence, suggest that we have some very powerful inner resources at our disposal.

Throughout history, whenever someone has discovered a new resource, we have always rushed to harness it for our benefit. For some reason, the one resource that hasn't been fully recognized or developed is the power residing in our own minds. Perhaps it is time that we recognize it and begin to release this power for our benefit.

Since the early 1970's, Win Wenger has been developing methods aimed at achieving this goal. A simple yet powerful process called Image-Streaming stands out as one of the processes that will help you tap into these powerful inner resources. Since its initial release, numerous applications have extended the value of Image-Streaming. New applications continue to be released as they are developed.

The power of Image-Streaming resides in the fact that it enables you to bridge your conscious and beyond-conscious minds. It can help you solve those nagging problems for which you cannot provide ready, logical answers. You can use Image-Streaming in learning or reading to improve your efficiency and effectiveness for understanding or mastering a book, a lecture, or some other subject. Image-Streaming by itself may increase your measurable IQ with accumulated practice.

Image-Streaming

You can achieve immediate success with Image-Streaming, and this success will improve with time. Image-Streaming can be a stand-alone process, or it can be integrated into more structured processes. After practicing Image-Streaming for only a short period of time, you will become more perceptive, more creative, and more intuitive. Image-Streaming provides a foundation for developing and exhibiting your own *genius*.

A Guaranteed Way to Improve Your Intelligence

Image-Streaming combines aspects of both Einstein's Deep-Thought Discovery Method and the Socratic Method for teaching and learning. Historically, these two methods have been closely associated with extraordinarily high levels of mental performance.

Einstein's Deep-Thought Discovery Method is based upon Albert Einstein's creative thought process.

Einstein used an active, internal visualization process to create and develop his ideas. He would let mental imagery play freely and examine it to see what he could learn.

He used this method to identify the principles of relativity. He once said, "Words or language…do not seem to play any role in my mechanism of thought. My elements of thought are …images…"[1]

Einstein was not the first scientist to use visualization, but he was the first respected scientist to inform the public about it.

More recently, the Nobel Prize-winning physicist, Richard Feynman, used imagery and noted, "In certain problems that I have done, it was necessary to continue the development of the picture as the method, before the mathematics could really be done."[2]

---

[1] *Opening the Mind's Eye,* by Ian Robertson, p. 84, St Martin's Press.
[2] *Sparks of Genius — The 13 Thinking Tools of the World's Most Creative People,* by Robert and Michele Root-Berstein, p.5, First Mariner Books, 2001.

Introduction

The Socratic Method, by contrast, focuses upon the use of language. The Socratic Method was developed and used in the first schools built in our modern tradition.

These first schools did not exist for the students alone. Leading thinkers of the time used these early schools to better develop their thoughts and perceptions by describing them to a group of avid listeners.

Subsequently, some thinkers, especially the Sophists and, most important, Socrates, began to use the platform of these schools to draw out ideas from their listeners.

This *drawing out* process proved so productive for creating leaps in understanding that education itself was named after it: *educare* (L.), "to draw forth."

When we look beyond the rigorous argument and dialog of the original Socratic Method, we can see what this process accomplished. It made people examine closely their inner and outer perceptions and respond to or describe what they discovered there.

Inherent in this experience is the idea that, "Whatever you focus upon, examine, and describe in detail to a listener, you will discover more and more about."

This idea is consistent with the Law of Effect from psychology that concludes, "You get more of what you reinforce." When you describe your own perceptions, you reinforce the behavior of being perceptive. When the Socratic Method was used in classical Greece and the European Renaissance, these tiny population centers produced a much higher ratio of geniuses than we have today.

When we combine the Socratic Method with the Einstein Deep Thought Discovery Method, as we do in Image-Streaming, we suddenly have something much more. We have a sensitive, synergistic process that delves deeply into our personal symbology in an intensifying, vivid experience of free-flowing imagery.

This free-flowing imagery not only opens up a wealth of insight and understanding to us, but it reinforces and builds whatever intelligence we have online.

As you proceed with Image-Streaming, you will find that it:

Image-Streaming

- Provides you with the opportunity to further your understanding of yourself, those important to you, and the world around you;
- Helps you identify what *is* really going on with you;
- Is a tool for creative problem-solving;
- Profoundly accelerates and improves learning;
- Supports innovation, creation, and invention;
- Provides a fast road to scientific discoveries;
- Increases intuition;
- Makes it easier to find *lost* items;
- Helps you gain control of your autonomic physiological processes;
- Is highly entertaining.

Over the years, we have found that more than 99% of the individuals who try Image-Streaming are successful in learning and practicing some form of it. These individuals profited immediately from the benefits of Image-Streaming!

Image-Streaming: How It Builds Intelligence

In the movie, *Phenomenon*, John Travolta stars as George Mailey, a small-town mechanic living in southern California. On the night of his 37th birthday, George is knocked to the ground by a mysterious, blinding light.

In the days that follow, George finds himself becoming more perceptive, more intelligent, more curious, more creative, and more enthusiastic.

Several weeks later, during a stressful confrontation at a local fair, George collapses and is taken to a hospital where a series of tests are run to find what has caused his collapse and the sudden, miraculous changes in him. George's brain scan indicates that there are far more regions active in his brain than his doctors have seen in anyone previously. His doctors explain that this accounts for the recent

Introduction

changes in his mental abilities. Although this story is fiction, there is a kernel of truth in it.

The key to building intelligence is to get widely different and separate regions of the brain to work more closely together. In his investigation of intelligence, John Ertl used an EEG brainwave analyzer and developed the most physiological IQ test ever devised. He found that intelligence is usually high when the left and right sides of the brain have a tightly knit phase relationship (the time interval between the stimulation of one side of the brain and obtaining a response on the other side), and low when they do not. Experience indicates that the same characteristic may be true for the front and back and the top and bottom of the brain.

If we want to build our intelligence, how can we put this knowledge to use in a practical methodology?

For millions of years, people have responded very quickly to external sensory information. For example, if someone suddenly yells, "TIGER," we will respond quite quickly. We may drop to the ground, run, or grab a weapon. In contrast, for internal perceptions, such as adjusting for a cramped position or developing a gradual feeling about a situation, we are not subject to the same pressure for speed. If we rely on our internal communications to form bridges across our brain to address any single event, we may find that one region completes its activities before another region even receives information.

Based upon our typical experience with the tiger, we have found that we can bypass this weakness in our internal communications by *simultaneously* involving as *many* of our senses as possible during an event. If we do this, we will establish two key conditions that provide critical benefits:

1. We will stimulate more widely different and separate regions of the brain simultaneously, and
2. We will activate these regions of the brain far more quickly, since they are associated with our external perceptions.

Whenever we establish these conditions, more regions of our brain come into closer phase relationships. As a result, we will enhance our active intelligence. We refer to this process as pole-bridging.

Image-Streaming

How can we easily and realistically establish these conditions in order to take advantage of the benefits?

Two of the most powerful pole-bridging activities include sight-reading while playing music (especially for children) and Image-Streaming.

Of the two activities, Image-Streaming is easier to learn and more convenient to use. Image-Streaming draws out subtle awarenesses from all over the brain, sorts them with the right temporal lobe as imagery, and describes them using the left temporal language ability. While Image-Streaming, you may find that you get more out of every experience by recognizing new or different aspects of it.

Image-Streaming and its applications have been recognized by others for their intrinsic value and have been included or referenced in the following books or programs:

- Spencer Westwood in an ebook, *Improving Your Guitar Playing*.
- Adelaide Bry in her excellent book, *Visualization: Directing the Movies of Your Mind*.
- Dr. Sidney J. Parnes, co-creator of the Osborn-Parnes Creative Problem-Solving method that launched the world-wide creativity movement, in his book: *Visionizing: State-of-the-Art Techniques for Encouraging Innovative Excellence* (Buffalo, NY: Creative Education Foundation, 1988).
- Dr. Sidney J. Parnes included an article from the *Journal of Creative Behavior* titled "Creative Creativity," that includes a version of the Beachhead discovery-making procedure, in his *Source Book for Creative Problem-Solving — A Fifty-Year Digest of Proven Innovative Processes* (Creative Education Foundation, 1992).
- Chris Brewer and Don G. Campbell, *Rhythms of Learning: Creative Tools for Lifelong Learning* (Tucson, AZ: Zephyr Press, 1991).
- Chris Brewer, *Freedom to Fly: 101 Activities for Building Self-Worth* (Tucson, AZ: Zephyr Press, 1993).

Introduction

- Paul Scheele's PhotoReading and Memory Optimizer programs from Learning Strategies.
- Lynn Schroeder and Sheila Ostrander in their three books, *Superlearning*; *Supermemory: The Revolution*; and *Superlearning 2000* (NY: Delacourte Press).
- Michael Gelb in his bestseller, *Discover Your Genius: How to Think Like History's Ten Most Revolutionary Minds* (NY: Harper Collins).
- Joe Vitale in one of his high-calibre books on emarketing.
- Cecil McGregor, on his website, in an article combining NLP's presuppositional techniques with Image-Streaming.
- Ronald Gross, *Peak Learning* (New York, NY: Jeremy P. Tarcher/Putnam, 1999).

Chapter 1:

You Are Brighter Than You Think

You were born thinking in images. For years, that was how you thought, perceived, and understood the world. When parents and teachers told you to stop daydreaming or stop looking out the window and pay attention, this powerful mode of thinking did not go away. It merely went underground. This mode of thinking is still available to you today and is very useful for increasing your creativity, crystallizing your understandings, and solving complex problems.

It is time now to rediscover the power of your images and to enhance your daily life with a technique that releases your powerful inner resources. Here are the instructions for receptive visual thinking or *Image-Streaming*.

Image-Streaming: The Process

Key Essentials

Before we start a description of the process, let's review the three characteristics essential for best results when Image-Streaming:

- Speak aloud to a listener or into a tape/digital voice recorder in a continuous, rapid-flow, full sensory description.
- Use the present tense.
- Describe an image using all of your sensory modes: visual, auditory, kinesthetic (including tactile awareness), gustatory, and olfactory.

Describing your images aloud will bring more of your images into your conscious awareness. This activity will help bridge the gap between the left and right sides of your brain. If you are Image-Streaming to answer a question or solve a problem, the images may seem unrelated to the question or context at first. But, once you let your images flow freely, you'll find that what you've been describing was amazingly and ingeniously accurate, providing you with the correct answer or a key insight. Describe your images using complete sentences. Just as the grammar of his Greek language gave Aristotle logic, the structure of our English language acts as a kind of Socratic questionnaire that is activated when we make our descriptions in complete sentences.

By using the present tense, you will reinforce your creation of an image. The more you describe something, the more of it you will get. It's even acceptable to make up a description while Image-Streaming to keep it going. This is your beyond-conscious mind at work. This action will feed your image. Using the present tense makes the Image-Stream more immediate and lasting.

Your brain is organized such that input from your senses is processed in different regions. Using all of the sensory modes in your description will quickly activate more regions of your brain. To promote your use of sensory description, review the section titled *Sensory Attributes* later in this chapter for examples of attributes that you can look for or observe in your images.

Hear
See
Smell
Taste
Touch

Image-Streaming

Preparation

Have either a tape/voice recorder or a listener available before you start. When you are first learning to Image-Stream, it is best to find a place where you and your partner will not be disturbed. Before your first attempts at Image-Streaming, do some *Velvety-Smooth Breathing* (see Appendix A) for two to three minutes to help you relax. After gaining some experience with the process, you will find that you can start Image-Streaming almost immediately without any special preparation. In fact, you will find that you can Image-Stream practically anywhere or anytime.

Image-Streaming Procedure

1. ***Sit back, close your eyes, and relax.*** You may want to do a little *Velvety-Smooth Breathing* (see Appendix A) to get more relaxed.
2. ***Start to Image-Stream.*** Describe aloud to your listener or voice recorder whatever images come to mind.[3] Go with your first or most immediate impressions and describe these images or impressions aloud. Describe them as rapidly as possible in a sustained flow of richly textured sensory detail. Make it a brainstorm of description, not of ideas but of adjectives that describe the image or images. More images will emerge as you continue to describe. Be alert for new images or changes and describe them when they happen. You do not need to create an orderly story in your description. Simply describe your stream of images as you notice them, using all five senses: visual, auditory, kinesthetic, olfactory, and gustatory.

Let yourself be surprised by what the images reveal to you. The more surprising those images are, the more likely that

---

[3] If you have difficulty in starting images, read the section, *Prompting Techniques,* found later in this chapter, and take advantage of the variety of techniques provided in Appendix C.

12

You Are Brighter Than You Think

you're getting fresh input from your inner, more comprehensive and accurate resources.

3. **Debrief** by going back through the experience. This step is optional, but it helps to reinforce your experience. Debriefing can provide you with new insights into your Image-Stream. It often elicits secondary thoughts, associations, or awarenesses that were not immediately apparent to you. Summarize this whole experience to another person, in a notebook, or on a computer. Changing the medium that you use for debriefing will give you the best results. See the section titled *Record and Learn from Your Experiences* later in this chapter for information on documenting your debriefing experience.

That's it! Image-Streaming is a simple process. It's easy to learn, but it can have a dramatic effect on your life.

If you find it difficult to obtain images at first, try the techniques introduced in *Prompting Techniques to Start Your Image-Stream* found later in this chapter and expanded upon in Appendix C.

Once you have found that you can start your images spontaneously, practice Image-Streaming at least ten minutes each day for ten days. Try some of the methods presented in the section titled *Building and Enhancing Your Image-Stream* during this period.

If, at the end of those ten days, your life isn't remarkably improved in various ways, then ignore everything we've said and go to some other system. Is this a fair test?

But, if your life is improved by the end of the ten days, continue practicing Image-Streaming for at least ten minutes each day. After twenty-one days, the gains will have become permanent. With continuing practice, your future experiences will get even better!

In summary, the Image-Streaming process consists of three brief steps:

- **Close your eyes** and relax.
- **Describe** your images as rapidly as possible in a sustained flow of richly textured sensory detail to a listener or recorder.
- **Debrief** to a different medium.

Image-Streaming

"Co-Tripping" with a Partner

Partner Image-Streaming is both good for you and highly recreational. It is a great experience to share with a friend, and it is especially recreational with a friend if you both visualize well.

To begin, both of you close your eyes while one of you starts describing your images to the other. It doesn't matter which one of you starts. Both of you should keep your eyes closed even when the other is talking.

One of you describes your own experience for a few sentences. When the speaker pauses for a breath, the other one rushes in with his or her description. When the new speaker pauses for breath, you rush back in with more of your own descriptions. Once both of your streams are started, don't allow any gap in this ongoing description. Make the experience one continuous flow of descriptive language and images.

When you are actively describing your images with a partner and alternating descriptive experiences, it is easy to be influenced by what your partner is describing. We encourage people to stay with their own imagery. Just be present so that your partner has someone to describe to. It is easy for you and your partner to enter each other's experiences, reacting to features in the other's experience, including features that are there but not yet described.

No matter what the cause of this response, we encourage people to stay with their own images, since they are receiving messages in their own symbolic code. This makes for more accurate messages and subsequent self-interpretation. Each person's inner imagery and symbolism has been differentiated by a lifetime of experience from that of the partner.

After completing this experience, discuss your impressions of the experience with your partner.

Insomniac's Special

One of the easiest ways to ensure going to sleep is to begin looking at your stream of spontaneous images without describing them or talking ...zzzz!

It's all the more reason to describe these images aloud to develop your awareness of them and of the understandings behind them.

The Creativity Break

The *Creativity Break* helps you become more creative, and it can improve your sense of well-being and make your afternoons fresher and more productive than your mornings – all for only a few minutes pleasantly invested each day.

Sometime between 11 a.m. and 2 p.m., Image-Stream for ten to fifteen minutes in the Gravity Position. This form of constructive respite will clear your head and nourish your brain.

Gravity Position: Lie flat on your back on the floor, without a pillow, and support your raised feet and lower legs on the seat of a chair or sofa. Support your legs up to the knees so as not to stress them, but not so high on the knee as to impede circulation. Loosen any tight clothes. Once you're comfortable, luxuriate in several deep, rewarding sighs. Then proceed to describe your images to a recorder or listener.

When you finish, get up slowly to adjust to the changes in your body. Your initial hesitation upon rising will quickly turn into a new

Image-Streaming

lightness and clarity. The pole-bridging accomplished while Image-Streaming, reinforced by better circulation to your brain from the Gravity Position, will enrich and extend your mental processes for a more productive afternoon.

Writer's Block – Fiction[4]

A writer of fiction once asked Win whether he should Image-Stream to record his entire novel before writing it. In response, Win suggested that he combine Image-Streaming with several other known techniques to help a writer, as follows:

- Image-Stream to computer or recorder without worrying about a story line. Just Image-Stream with the intent of being shown interesting scenes from the story-to-be. Let the scenes surprise you.
- Write in high-intensity bursts, not a dribble a day as most people tell you. Write in such high-volume, high-intensity bursts that your characters seem to take over the story and carry it in unexpected directions.
- Never stall out with writer's block – just Image-Stream and describe the images that may become the next point in your story line. Let yourself flow into a character, the plot line, or any development that may come up after what might have been your block. You want to generate a lot of stuff so that you can throw a lot of it away in order to get to the good stuff.
- See if you can identify with each of your different characters. Perhaps try a *Borrowed Genius* exercise (see Appendix D) with each character to get inside of each character to find out why he or she did this or that.
- When you think you are done, ask your Image-Stream what key consideration or factor you left out that you need to

---

[4] See the Core Book by Win Wenger with Mark Bossert, *End Writer's Block Forever.*

consider. In your story, explore what you can say through implication rather than spelling it out for the reader. Put the reader to work!

If the reader is forced to figure out what has happened, he will experience more emotional impact than if you clearly spelled out the "death" scene in gory detail.

- Early on, ask your Image-Stream what your goals are for the story beyond getting it written and read. What is the transcendent point that this story can make?
- One of the most valuable contributions your Image-Stream can make is in supplying visual and sensory detail to the various scenes and actions. Your Image-Stream will not provide explicit prose, but it can offer various images that you can use to lace the story to bring it alive in the reader's mind.
- Early on, and perhaps at intervals, use the *Toolbuilder* procedure (see Appendix D) to experience a highly advanced civilization where everyone writes fiction so brilliantly that back here on Earth he would be considered a genius author. Learn from this civilization how everyone came to make this happen. Use this knowledge to your advantage.
- Use the *Borrowed Genius* procedure (see Appendix D) to take on the persona of a genius author and use this experience to resolve any sections of the story that you find difficult to write.
- Lastly, use bursts of *Freenoting* and *Windtunnel* (see Appendix D). Once you establish a strong flow, it's amazing how you will enrich your writing process.

These are only a few of the ways to use Project Renaissance methods to get that story or novel of yours well written. Use whatever suggestions will be helpful to you.

Writer's Block – Non-Fiction

Most of what is in the curriculum for fiction writers applies here also. This is especially true of using Image-Streaming to immediately get past any writer's block or a "waiting-for-inspiration" period. In

Image-Streaming

addition, try any of the following suggestions described for developing your essay or book:

- Peter Elbow suggested in *Writing Without Teachers* that an author should write an essay to its conclusion. Then take that conclusion and make it the starting point for a fresh essay. Write a fresh essay through to a conclusion. Then take that conclusion and make it the starting point for writing another fresh essay through to a conclusion. After several of these cycles, you probably have something pretty substantial to say.

- Ask, "What's the most important thing I have to say here?" Take the most important thing in your essay and ask yourself, "Why is that important to me?" Pause and write down your answer. To whatever you've written down as your answer, ask again, "Why is that important to me?" Pause, and write down your new answer. Then ask again about this new answer, "Why is this important to me?" Go through this cycle seven times or more and see where this leads you.[5]

- At the conclusion of your essay or non-fiction report, ask yourself, "What key thing did I leave out?" Ask your Image-Stream this question and simply let yourself be shown the answer. Describe aloud for several minutes or until you have an "aha!" Then, decide whether what you've been shown is important enough for you to include in your essay. Repeat this procedure as needed until your project is dynamite!

- Let your Image-Stream provide you with a picture that shows you the concept that you are writing about. Play with the picture. Describe it. See if you don't have a clearer, more interesting way to describe that concept than before.

- How to open your discourse? Much the same as for getting around Writer's Block.

---

[5] This procedure for digging through to the essentials was borrowed from a somewhat different usage in NLP and attributed to Virginia Satir.

- How to work such and such an effect at various points during your papers? Ask your Image-Stream, describe in detail whatever comes, and you will usually find it presenting you with a superb way to proceed.

Besides these useful exercises, you may find that your Image-Stream can help you to locate data needed for completion of your project.

Prompting Techniques

Virtually everyone can quickly and readily learn to *get pictures* in their mind's eye. If you are one of those individuals who didn't immediately get images and would like some help getting started, here are some ideas. We provide a series of *prompting techniques* to ensure that you can *get pictures* and realize that you *are* able to think visually.

When you are having trouble getting started, try the *Helper Technique* below, or any one of the 22 additional techniques described in Appendix C, for a sustained 10- to 20-minute period. If this effort does not lead you into more interesting images, try another technique. It is truly rare to find anyone who has run the gamut of these techniques without getting pictures in their mind's eye.

Once you have a technique that works, use that approach to start your Image-Stream and continue describing your *pictures*. Do not waste time trying out other prompting techniques, since that would just slow down your practice. What matters is the Image-Stream itself, not how you got it started.

Working with a Listener

Prompting techniques work best if you have a listener who can watch your *attention cues,* such as changes in your breathing patterns, or eye-movements beneath your closed eyelids. Whenever any such cue indicates some response within you, the Listener should immediately ask you, "What was in your awareness just then?" This will help you notice when these images happen and will start the flow of description going. In each of these techniques, we will refer to the person seeking to see images as the Image-Streamer and the assisting partner as the Listener.

Image-Streaming

What follows is the description of one such prompting technique. Refer to Appendix C for additional techniques if you do not have a partner to assist you or if the *Helper Technique* does not provide you with the desired results.

Helper Technique for Starting Your Image-Stream

For this technique you need a partner to follow these instructions with you.

Though your imagery goes on all the time, some images come through a little stronger than other images. When this happens, you unconsciously make little responses that are visible to observers. You make these responses when you start to give attention to some stimulus.

These little responses are *attention cues*. The Listener observing an attention cue should gently ask, "What was in your awareness just then?" Repeat this until the Image-Streamer realizes he or she *was* seeing something and should be able to begin the flow of description from that point.

To assist the untrained Listener, here are two attention cues that are highly visible and obvious:

- When you start to give attention to something, you hold your breath. If the Image-Streamer is instructed to breathe slowly, smoothly, and continuously, with no pauses between breathing in and breathing out, then a pause in breathing becomes highly visible by contrast and an occasion for asking the Image-Streamer, "What was in your awareness just then?"

- If the Image-Streamer keeps eyes closed and the Listener notices them moving around under the lids, what are they looking at? Eye movement under the closed lids is significant, not just eyelid flutter. When you spot eye movement, ask the Image-Streamer, "What was in your awareness just then?" When in doubt as to either cue, go ahead and ask the question.

The Image-Streamer, when noticing any images, should go ahead and start describing them instead of waiting for the Listener to ask, "What was in your awareness just then?"

Once anything at all is spotted, the Image-Streamer should describe in as much detail as possible, even forcing some made-up detail if need be, to get the flow started. The Listener should not interrupt the flow of description and images once it is started. Once started, more imagery will come and, shortly, the Image-Streamer will truly enjoy reporting the increasingly meaningful and intriguing internal events.

This spotting and identifying of attention cues is the preferred way to get Image-Streaming started if you were not able to simply look in and self-start. If the Listener has been observing for attention cues for 10 minutes, and the Image-Streamer still does not start the Image-Stream, switch to one of the alternative methods described in Appendix C.

We predict that once you read the examples in Appendix C, you will be able easily to think of hundreds of other such devices for triggering a flow of images without directing the images themselves.

The objective for each prompting technique is to ensure that visual imagery happens. Once you discover any kind of impression at all, "describe the dickens out of it" as if it were still in view, until more appears. Keep finding fresh things to say about it, even if it's long gone, until more appears.

The ideal discovery-state and the ideal personal-growth state is the process of rapidly describing, in rich, accurate detail, the flow of visual mental images. These mental images are undirected except for their interaction with your rich assortment of beyond-conscious understandings and perceptions.

The ability to Image-Stream is natural. The difficulty some people initially have is learned or artificial. Children don't have any difficulty seeing their inner images. The highest incidence of people having difficulty getting images is among people who have trained other people in imagery or in various forms of meditation! It is rare to have someone go through all of the above back-up procedures without getting images. It is rare indeed!

It doesn't matter how you get the rapid flow of detailed, sensorily rich description going. Once you have your Image-Stream going, you will find it much more rewarding to report actual ongoing inner

Image-Streaming

phenomena than "just making up a story." Over time, the accumulated effect of Image-Streaming will make everyone into a highly efficient, sensitive, accurate observer, not only of their inner imagery, but also of their interior and exterior senses. It's getting the richly textured flow of describing started, and keeping it going without interruption, pause or much repetition, that's important. The rest will naturally take care of itself.

Sensory Attributes

Often people have a special preference for perceiving information through one of their senses. While Image-Streaming, you obtain the best results when you activate as many regions in your mind as possible. Addressing as many of your senses as possible in your descriptions will activate new poles.

To help stimulate your memory with the type of information that can be described through your senses, review the examples provided in the following tables. The tables include some specific examples and some general characteristics that you can use to guide you to more specific details. If you include detailed, specific, sensory-based observations in your description, you will find yourself noticing more and more detail in your images.

Gustatory Attributes with Examples			
Sweet	Fruit-like...	Spices...	Drinks...
Sour	...apple	...cinnamon	...mint tea
Salty	...blueberries	...curry	...root beer
Tangy	...banana	...mint	...pina colata
Bitter	...	...rosemary	
Fermented	Other foods...	...pepper	...hot chocolate
...	....	...	...coffee
			...

You Are Brighter Than You Think

Visual Attributes with Examples

Color…	Texture…	Posture…	Size…
…blue	…rough	…erect	…high
…green	…smooth	…slouching	…wide
…burgundy	…silky	…lying flat	…bulky
…swirls of…	…bumpy	…sitting	…thin
…with highlights..	…fur-like	…stooped	…fat
…	…	…	…
Brightness…	Perspective…	Reflective…	Motion…
…dim/dull	…looking down	…shiny	…like a shot
…blinding	…looking up	…mirror-like	…slow
…twilight	…close-up	…dull	…30 mph
…shining	…distant	…sparkling	…smooth
…sparkling	…from inside	…glossy	…jerky
…	…	…	…
Clarity…	Looks like…	Shape….	Time…
…hazy	…plant…	…round	…old
…crystal clear	…animal…	…square	…new
…translucent	…object…	…sharp	…ancient
…foggy	…place…	…sloping	…futuristic
…mottled	…material…	…blob	…prior
…spattered	…insect…	…silhouette…	…later
…	…	…	…

Add your own examples to these lists.

Image-Streaming

Auditory Attributes with Examples

Volume...	Quality...	Location...	Tonality...
...loud	...gruff	...behind	...echo
...soft	...screech	...in front	...resonance
...whispering	... squeak	...all around	...
...deafening	... grunt	...far away	
...fading	...crackle	...	Emotions...
...	...pop		...angry
	...bang	Timing...	...depressed
Pitch...	...whining	...burst	...excited
...high	...grinding	...increasing	...happy
...low	...scratch	...decreasing	...calm
...flat	...shrill	...drawn out	...agitated
...sharp	...scream	...rhythmic	...bored
...	...	...	...

Olfactory Attributes with Examples

Flower-like...	Chemical-like...	Spices...	Rotting
...roses	...ammonia	...cinnamon	Musty
...lilac	...chlorine	...curry	Rancid
...	...gasoline	...mint	Sweet
	...tar	...pepper	Pungent
Food-like...	...perfume	...vanilla	Sweaty
...hot bread	...ozone		Smoky
...grilled steak		Drinks...	Musky
...fish	Nature...	...coffee	
...banana	...mown hay	... hot cocoa	
...garlic	...sulphur spring	...orange juice	
...	...	...	

Kinesthetic Attributes with Examples			
Texture…	Emotions…	Environment…	Movement…
….soft	…angry	…humidity	…speed
…rough	…depressed	…temperature	…direction
…velvety	…excited	…wind	…vibration
…satiny	…joyous	…rain	…falling
…gritty	…frustrated	…sunshine	…
…furry	…tired	…hot	
…hard	…happy	…cold	Body…
…coarse	…loving	…	…hunger
…hot/cold	…fearful		…thirst
…scratchy	…calm	Weight…	…pain
…slimy	…pleased	…heavy	…exhaustion
…smooth	…restless	…floating	…position
…slippery	…impatient	…light	…balance
…	…	…	…

Building and Enhancing Your Image-Stream

There are a number of simple exercises that you can do for building or enhancing your Image-Streaming abilities.

If you are just starting, experiment with holding an object in your hands. With your eyes *open*, describe the object in detail, using all of your sensory inputs, speaking as quickly as possible for two to three minutes, up to five minutes if you have the time. Do this several times.

After trying this exercise one or more times, *close* your eyes, and describe some other familiar object in detail, such as an apple, a bottle, or a cereal box. Use all of your sensory inputs, speaking as quickly as possible for two to three minutes, up to five minutes if you have the

Image-Streaming

time. Several trials of this will prepare you more readily for describing your spontaneous images.

To summarize, the following criteria are critical in developing your Image-Stream:

- Keep your eyes continuously closed during the process.
- Describe aloud in compelling, rich sensory detail.
- Maintain a high-volume flow of such description, regardless of whether you think you have anything worth describing.

Beyond these basic requirements, here are some additional ways to improve the qualities of your experience in Image-Streaming and to strengthen your contact with the resources that your Image-Stream represents:

- Panoramic Scan Technique — From your present location in your image, turn slowly a full 360 degrees in small incremental steps and describe what you see as you turn.
- Sensory awareness — Proceed through each of your five senses, including your perceptions related to each one in your description; see the table in *Sensory Attributes* above as a reminder for things to observe and describe.
- Move around — Physically move around in your image and examine whatever new images come into your field of view.
- Point of view — Change your viewing perspective; move out, move in, move up, move down, move in a variety of directions and describe what is encountered.

Yolaine Stout has provided a suggestion to prepare you for a more productive Image-Streaming session. She recommends a procedure that is intended to activate your awareness of all your senses prior to visualizing. Once you follow this procedure, then you can let your senses adjust to the changing visualization.

Before you start Image-Streaming, relax and go through the following steps:

1. Become aware of your breath — adjust your breathing to a deep, rhythmic pattern.
2. Become aware of physical sensations (weight of your body, air currents, tingling, warmth, or coolness) — magnify those sensations, or alter them. Try feeling lighter, heavier, cooler, or warmer. Make your hands tingle and make them stop tingling.
3. Become aware of inner sounds (sounds of swallowing, breathing, or your heart pumping). Then move to outer sounds such as the wind howling, raindrops falling, or the sound of someone calling your name.
4. Become aware of any taste in your mouth — imagine the taste of warm cocoa or a cup of hot coffee.
5. Become aware of any smells around you — imagine smelling that warm cocoa or hot coffee.
6. See the cup of warm cocoa or hot coffee in exquisite detail.
7. Feel the emotion of the experience.
8. Integrate these senses into a multi-sensory event such as the memory of hunger, someone cooking a grand feast, being called to eat, and sitting down to eat, tasting the food and feeling the experience.

Try this process before your next Image-Streaming exercise and note the effect.

An interesting variation to your routine Image-Streaming is based upon an article by R. W. Peters.[6] He reported that feeding back one's own voice directly from a microphone through a stereo headset, without delay, speeded and clarified not only one's speech but also one's thinking. He discovered that this effect lasted for hours afterward. With today's stereo equipment or personal computers, many of us have the means to set up this feedback path in our homes. Try Image-Streaming while receiving direct audio feedback through a headset. Most of today's digital voice recorders include this feature.

Experiment with any of these techniques while describing your images.

---

[6] "The Effects of Changes in Side-Tone Delay and Level upon the Rate of Oral Reading of Normal Speakers," by R. W. Peters in the *Journal of Speech and Hearing Disorders*, XIX, 1954.

Image-Streaming

Record and Learn from Your Experiences

Appendix B provides a typical example of a self-report form. This form is for your private use. It is intended to help you debrief after an Image-Streaming session. It also lets you record, retrieve, and review your progress or changes in your Image-Streaming experiences. Adapt the form to fit your own needs.

When you use the form, we suggest that you leave off the title until you have a dozen or more experiences recorded. Then, sort these experiences into categories and name each experience accordingly. You now have an easy way to retrieve information concerning your past experiences.

If you record your experiences on a computer, you will be able to search through these records at a later time using the built-in search feature on your computer. Be sure that you have entered several keywords that uniquely characterize each particular experience in each file that you save. This will enable you to search old records of experiences by date or keywords and review these experiences, possibly discovering patterns or new ideas in the process.

If you keep the recorded tapes from your Image-Streaming sessions instead of reusing them, attach your self-report form to the tape and place the title or titles on the package so that you can easily see them. If you save the forms, you may find trends or patterns on the forms and in your experiences. This is especially true of the check marks for *Sensory Data* that may indicate possible biorhythms or other patterns.

Please answer each item as frankly and objectively as you can, reinforcing your perceptiveness as much as possible. Completing this form is only one way to debrief, but don't let this or any particular format slow you down or get in the way of your Image-Streaming.

The search for meaning immediately after an experience may induce almost as much pole-bridging in the brain as the original experience. Therefore, completing this form may enhance your experience. You may find another, more convenient method for debriefing. As long as the medium that you use to debrief is different from your Image-Streaming experience, it will help to further your understanding of your experiences.

Chapter 2: Creative Problem-Solving

When do we have to be creative in problem-solving? If your problem could be solved in a logical manner based upon what you consciously know, isn't there a good chance that you would have solved it already? For example, if you need to design a stronger bridge, you could increase the size and weight of the supporting structure. This is a straightforward, logical solution to the design problem. But if you want to design a stronger bridge while making it lighter, your present knowledge may not necessarily lead you to a straightforward logical solution.

If you haven't yet solved your problem, most likely we are dealing with a problem that cannot be solved logically based upon what we *know* about it! In fact, what we *know* often becomes the problem in finding a solution. What we *know* can get in the way of fresh ideas, concepts, or the perceptions that we need for finding an answer!

It is usually in images that the most reliable answers to questions appear. Your conscious thinking has been limited by the ability of your language to represent the world. If an answer to a question comes in words, did it come from these rich inner resources or did it come from the limited, verbally focused part of our brain where we get the same old answers? If an answer comes in images, especially if they are a surprise, we have an excellent indicator that we're getting data from somewhere else in our brains.

You have within your mind more information and resources than you realize. This store of information and the available resources can give you better answers to your problems than you ever dreamed possible. Your mind is a self-organizing device. It is constantly sorting through your perceptions and experiences, both consciously and unconsciously. It is assembling this information into organized, higher-order understandings. This happens no matter who you are or what you are doing.

To assist you in activating your available resources to tackle a difficult problem, we are going to introduce you to two basic problem-solving processes. The first process describes how you can extend your Image-Streaming experience and apply it to obtain answers to your questions or problems. The second process, *Over the Wall*, provides you with a variation of Image-Streaming that uses surprise to assist you in obtaining your sought-after answers. We expect that these processes will help improve your odds for solving many of the problems that you encounter.

Image-Streaming for Creative Problem-Solving

At every instant, our minds are reflexively sorting through all of our observations and perceptions. We think about what we are thinking about. And, we create images that best represent to us whatever is occurring at the present time.

If you have a problem that you want answered, you can redirect your thoughts from external stimuli to your internal resources by asking yourself a question or pointing to a problem. Then, through Image-Streaming, you can *let* your images provide you with the answers.

This process can be used any time that you plan on Image-Streaming. It will provide your mind and images a direction. If you want to experiment with this process and don't have a specific problem that you can readily identify, review the section later in this chapter titled *Finding Problems*. This section will help you identify problems that are specifically applicable to you. It also provides you with a sampling of more global problems that you can experiment with.

Once you have identified the problem and preferably written it down, proceed as follows:

1. ***The Question***: Ask yourself a question.

2. ***Start to Image-Stream:*** With a listener or recorder, sit back, relax, close your eyes, and describe aloud whatever images

come to mind. Go with your first or most immediate impressions and describe these images or impressions aloud, as rapidly as possible in a sustained flow of richly textured sensory detail. Make it a kind of brainstorm of description, not of ideas but of adjectives that describe the image or images.

More images will emerge as you continue to describe. Be alert for these new images or other changes and describe these when they happen.

You do not need to organize or create an orderly story in your description. Simply describe your stream of images as you notice them, using all five senses—visual, auditory, kinesthetic, olfactory, and gustatory.

Let yourself be surprised by what the images reveal to you. The more surprising, the more likely that you're getting fresh input from your subtler, more comprehensive and accurate resources.

After five to fifteen minutes of Image-Streaming, the answer to your question or problem often becomes obvious. If this happens, skip to the *Debrief* step below.

At other times, the answer is not as readily available or understood through your images. If this happens, follow the remaining steps to help you identify the meaning of your images.

3. *Feature Questioning:* While describing, pick one object from your image that attracts your attention, such as rock, a tree or a bush. Imagine laying a hand on that feature and studying its feel while describing it to strengthen your contact with that object.

Ask the object, "Why are you (meaning the object) here as part of my answer?" Or, "Why are you here as part of this message for me?" See if the imagery changes when you ask that question. Describe the changes.

4. *Inductive Inference:* Once you've described your images for five to fifteen minutes, thank your Image-Streaming faculties for showing you this answer. Then ask their help in

Image-Streaming

understanding this answer or message.[7] Ask for an entirely different set of images that somehow still give you the same answer to the same problem. Then describe the new images for an additional two to three minutes. After this, ask for a third set of images for just a minute or so that still show the same answer or message in an entirely different way!

- *What's the same?* Review your sets of images and identify what is the same in each set. Maybe it's the color green. Maybe it's a triangular-shaped object. Maybe it's just a feeling. Identify the common elements in your images. The similarities represent the core of the message after all the ornamentation has been swept aside. These themes or common elements are your core answer or message.

The more detail you have from each of your several sets of images, the easier it is to find matches, themes, or common elements that let you make sense out of what you've seen.

This process can be visually represented as shown in the figure below. The center of the figure where all three circles overlap indicates the common area that you are seeking.

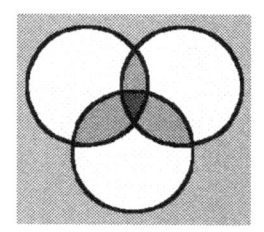

---

[7] It may be necessary to search for the meaning of your images (your answer), since your mind works mostly with sensory images instead of language. In fact, 40 times as much of the physical brain (70-90%) associates in sensory images as opposed to word-concepts (2%). Thus we may have to interpret or translate our sensory images in order to obtain our understandings and answers.

- *Relate*: Go back to your original question or context and determine in what way or ways these core elements provide the answer to your question.

5. ***Debrief*** by going back through the experience. Debriefing can provide you with new insights into your Image-Stream. It often elicits secondary thoughts, associations, or awarenesses that were not immediately apparent to you. Summarize this whole experience to another person, in a notebook, or on a computer. Changing the medium that you use for debriefing will give you the best results. See the section titled *Record and Learn from Your Experiences* later in this chapter for information on documenting your debriefing experience.

In most cases, you will find an answer to your question or problem after going through this sequence. If you have not found an answer, often you will have found additional insights that will help you pursue your answer.

If you have not found your answer or understood it, wait for a period of time and try the process again. When you try it again, reconsider the statement of the problem or question. Modifying how you state the problem or question can affect the answering process. Perhaps your original vision or understanding of the problem was too narrow; by broadening the answer space, you may now obtain an answer or a better answer.

One unique advantage of Image-Streaming is that nearly all other creative problem-solving methods invest much of their effort into redefining the question or problem, before they ever get started on finding answers. Even though you have stated your problem via a question at the beginning of this process, your deeper resources may already know what the real problem or question is, and they will immediately get on with giving you an answer.

Another advantage is the rapid results that are attainable. Even though the intelligence-building effects of Image-Streaming take time, you can get an answer in a minute or so with practice. This is useful when the answer is of more value than the incremental step in intelligence building.

Once you have an answer to your question or a solution to your problem, you may want to validate the results to assure yourself that the next actions that you take are appropriate. Some sort of validation is always recommended following any problem-solving process.

Validation

Even when some answers come through with seeming certainty, it's still a human instrument receiving them. This instrument is subject to distortion, deletions, and generalizations from previous life experiences. Thus, even if these interior processes do tend to be more accurate than other information processes, it behooves you to check their validity against other indicators, just as you would for information from any other source.

All of our potential creative solutions need to be validated, whatever their source. Compare the fields of human endeavor that have advanced in the last thousand years (notably empirical science and technology) with those that have not (notably politics and religion). For progress, we have to be willing to risk our beliefs and put matters to a test.

Don't hesitate to ask your inner processes questions such as:

- How can I make sure that I'm on the right track with this understanding? — Your imagery and awareness should give you either a way to test and validate, or a reminder of real data or experiences that demonstrate that this is the right answer.
- What more do I need to know in this context?
- How best can I test this to make sure it is so?
- What's a good, practical, first step to act upon with this understanding?

Be alert for opportunities to check your answers by other means as well, including conventionally gathered empirical and scientific evidence. It behooves you to pursue validation after any problem-solving session.

Creative Problem-Solving

In summary, the Image-Streaming process for problem-solving consists of the following steps:

- Select a **problem** or **question.**
- Close your eyes and relax. **Describe** your images as rapidly as possible in a sustained flow of richly textured sensory detail to a listener or recorder.
- **Feature Questioning.**
- **Inductive Inference.**
- **Debrief** to a different medium.
- **Validate** your answer.

You may stop whenever you feel that your problem has been solved or your question answered.

Over the Wall

Everyone has his or her own internal critic, editor, or squelcher. This is the part of your mind that rapidly evaluates information, events, or thoughts, and too often shuts down any new or creative ideas.

To come up with unique and creative ideas, you will find it necessary to bypass this internal critic. In order to accomplish this, most creative problem-solving methods use either speed or surprise. *Over the Wall* uses surprise to get you past your internal critic and into new territory.

Over the Wall uses a receptive visualization process (Image-Streaming), but it starts with a directed visualization.

The directed part consists of building an image of a beautiful garden, bounded on one side by a high wall. You are requested not to look beyond the wall while describing your garden. Beyond the wall is your Answer Space, the scene where your answer will be revealed to you. The whole process will give your powerful inner resources the opportunity to surprise you with new or unexpected images.

Image-Streaming

The garden provides:
- A running start for describing your internal experience.
- An experience of pleasure while stimulating more regions of your mind.
- A safe, quiet place, where you can simply relax into the pleasures of relating the experience, without concern over the problem that is being addressed at other levels of your mind.

The wall provides:
- A convenient screen, behind which a stage can be set by your inner resources for displaying answers without interference from your conscious mind.
- An opportunity for suddenness, a threshold device that you can cross over abruptly and be surprised by your first impression of the answer, regardless of any prior expectations.

The Answer Space is blocked from us by the wall but gives us access to entire worlds as the stage for our answers to be displayed.

Creative Problem-Solving

Choose a question

In preparation, choose some question or issue for which you would like to find the answer or resolution. The question can be related to your personal life, your career, your community, national or world problems, or even scientific or technical problems—so long as you passionately do want to find its answer.

This strong emotional impact is far more arousing to your powerful inner resources than some trivial or trick question would be.

If you need help in identifying problems to address, see *Finding Problems* later in this chapter.

You will get better results with *Over-the-Wall* on open-ended questions, as distinct from yes-or-no questions. For example, "What's the best way to earn a raise from my boss," instead of, "Should I ask my boss for a raise?" This gives your inner resources some room to work at showing you what they perceive in relation to your question.

You will obtain better results if the answer can be made into some sort of *win-win* situation, instead of resulting in someone's loss or harm. In the above example, both you and your boss *win*, as opposed to, "How can I extract a raise from my boss?" The more sensitive part of you takes so many more factors into account than your conscious mind can.

If you want to understand the key part of any new subject or if you simply want to improve your understanding of a subject, write a statement of just what it is that you are trying to understand. Then you can use the Answer Space on the far side of the wall in two ways:

- To obtain the key to understanding this matter (that you have just written out), by asking for that very key. Or,
- To obtain an answer to the question, "What is the key thing I need to understand in this context?"

Either of these approaches will give your inner resources the opportunity to provide your conscious mind the understanding that you seek.

If you haven't already, write down now your question or a statement of the problem that you want to address.

Image-Streaming

Have a listener

Have another person to work with during this voyage of discovery. Describe your impressions aloud to this external point of focus. Having an external point of focus makes a huge difference in outcome. With a listener, success in this procedure is highly probable. Without a listener, failure is virtually guaranteed!

If you do not have a listener readily available, do not let that stop you. Instead of a partner reading you these instructions and listening to your responses, you may record the instructions on a tape with appropriate gaps in the talking to allow time for a response.

When you play this tape, record your responses into another recorder. If you need more time than your gaps leave you, pause your instruction tape as necessary. Make sure that you are familiar with your player so that you do not need to open your eyes to pause or restart your player.

If you have neither a listener nor a second recorder for the instructions, a short form of *Over the Wall* is provided in a later section of this chapter.

It is recommended that your listener read the following instructions to you so you can keep your attention on the experience.

Step-by-step Instructions for *Over the Wall*

1. With your question identified, set it aside and don't give it any more conscious thought for awhile. Instead of confronting the question directly, give your more sensitive resources the opportunity to set up a space where the answer to that question will be on display for you. To screen the Answer Space from interference by what you *know* about the problem in your conscious mind, imagine that this Answer Space is hidden from your view by a great wall—a wall that you can't see past until you are beyond it yourself.

2. With your eyes closed, imagine that you are in a very beautiful garden, a garden that is extraordinarily lovely and very different from any that you've ever seen before. On the far side of your garden is the wall that blocks your view of the

Creative Problem-Solving

Answer Space. Beyond that wall, without further concern or effort from your conscious mind, a space is now being set for you to display the best answer to your question. On this side of the wall, you are in this exquisitely beautiful garden. Begin to describe this garden in a rapid, continuous description for five to ten minutes. Remember to use full sentences in your description to help further your focus on the details of your perceptions.

While describing the garden, it may help to pretend that you are a radio reporter, describing the location just before a scheduled event for your listening audience. Describe this garden in richly textured detail to your audience. Start with what is directly in front of you in the garden and proceed to describe the garden all around you. Make your listener see, feel, smell, hear, and taste the experience through the richness of your description.

3. Now, step up to the side of the wall and describe the wall in the same manner that you've been describing the garden. Don't peek at what is on the other side of that wall. Put your hand on the wall and study the feel of it. Lean your face up against it. Make the feel and smell of the wall, as well as its appearance, real to your listener.

While you are describing, notice when and if you get mental images in your mind's eye, as in a dream. If you see these images, switch to describing them even if they leave the garden, the wall, or the answer space. These other images may be a more direct route to your answer than going over the wall.

4. Don't peek! Suddenness is the key to catching your answer. We don't want your conscious *knowledge* about the question jumping in with, "No, that can't be it. The answer has to look like this!" The trick is to experience *jumping over the wall* so suddenly that you catch even yourself by surprise. Your objective is to catch by surprise whatever is on the other side of the wall and to be surprised by what you find.

Image-Streaming

When the time comes, you will describe your very first impression of what's on the far side of the wall. Describe that very first impression even if it seems unrelated or trivial at first. Describe this first impression regardless of what it is and whether it's a picture or just some sort of conceptual impression. The act of describing this first impression exposes your ingenious and unexpected answer. Sooner or later, you will discover enough information by describing your images to learn how this Answer Space provides you with an effective answer to your problem.

Jump **now**! Please start describing your first impressions. If you want, you can start by describing what you are wearing on your feet or what surface you are standing upon. The more surprised that you are at what shows up in your images, the more likely that you are obtaining fresh input from your more powerful inner resources instead of simply recycling what you already *know* in your conscious mind.

5. Continuing to explore and describe what you've found in the Answer Space. Is there some feature that especially attracts your attention? Describe that feature further, or select some particular feature here, such as a bush, tree, or side of a house, and ask it mentally, "Why are you here, in this context? How do you relate to this answer?" In what ways does your picture or impression change in response to your question? Describe this in detail. If you already fully understand the answer that has been shown to you, let's skip to Step #7. Otherwise let's continue with the next step.

6. Mentally thank your inner resources for showing you the answer to your question, but ask their help in understanding it. Find some object in your Answer Space that can serve as a screen, just as your garden wall did earlier. This can be the wall of a house, a closed door, or cover of a photo album, anything that fits the purpose of being a screen.

Without sneaking a peek, approach the screening object and lay your hand on it. Then ask your inner resources to show exactly the same answer to the same question as before, in an entirely different scene on the far side of the new screen.

Enter the new scene and describe it in detail. Then search for the similarities between the old and new pictures. Perhaps it is grass, the color blue, water, people running, or a certain feeling from both pictures. In effect you are creating a second Answer Space, with an entirely different scene in it. What is the same between the old and new pictures? These similarities somehow represent the answer that you are searching for.

7. Return to the here and now, feeling fully refreshed. Like an astronaut returning from a mission, debrief.

If you've been working with a listener, get a new listener, a recorder or notepad. If you've been working with a recorder, get a notepad. Use a different medium from what you were using for the original experience.

Describe a little of your garden experience, then describe in detail everything you can about when you jumped over the wall. During this retrospective, the action of describing is often the stage at which understandings and meanings click into place.

To help build relationships within your brain, use the present tense while debriefing even though the experience is already in the past. Once you have your answer, you may want to do some validation.

Did you get images from behind the wall before you crossed over it? This can happen and is all right. If you describe them now, they might be relevant or might be your inner resources' shortcut to show your answers. In any case, the repeated tease of "don't peek behind the wall" adds energy to what you experience once you do finally get to the Answer Space on the far side.

Short Form of Over the Wall

So that you can keep your eyes closed and don't have to keep looking at the instructions, here is a short form of *Over the Wall*. Describe, describe, describe in richly textured detail:

Image-Streaming

1. **The Garden.**
2. **The Wall.**
3. **The Answer Space** beyond that wall.
4. **Feature-questioning** — examine some particular aspect or feature in your Answer Space.
5. **New Scene** — same answer to same question, but shown differently.
6. **Debrief.**

Getting the Meaning from Your Images

Perhaps you have fully described your images but are still not able to determine consciously what they mean. As described under *Image-Streaming for Creative Problem-Solving* earlier in this chapter, *inductive inference* is one way to help you determine the meaning of your images.

These processes are necessary because as much as 40 times more of your physical brain (70-90%) associates in sensory images rather than in word-concepts (2%). Thus our initial understandings and answers occur in a different processing language—sensory images—where we encounter metaphors and need to interpret them.

Debriefing can also assist you in understanding your images. For inventions, technical or mechanical problems and art, answers received through *Over the Wall* are usually quite literal. For most other issues, the answer may be shown in some sort of metaphor, cartoon, parable, pun or simile because of the way your brain works. These images represent symbolism that is unique to your mind and experiences. In such cases it may take some effort to figure out consciously what your images are telling you.

The most important thing in determining your answer is to *not* try to figure it out until after you've let the whole experience unfold and after you've described it in detail. If your "aha!" insight hits you in mid-stream, well and good. This will happen more and more frequently as you repeat this process. However, searching for meanings before you've detailed your experience invites your conscious knowledge about the problem situation to come back and interfere with your more sensitive internal data. This may stop you short of seeing the answer.

Once your experience is fully described and recorded, your "data is out on the table." Your conscious search for meaning can no longer hide or distort it. Here are several ways to improve your chances of identifying the meaning of what you found over the wall:

- By describing the image in the most richly textured detail.
- By describing your image more rapidly and outrunning your internal editor, thus getting to the most meaningful part of the experience.
- By engaging more of your senses in the experience, by noticing and describing—through sight, touch, smell, movement, space, mass, temperature, texture, taste, feel, etc.—thus getting better contact with your more sensitive inner resources.
- After initially orienting to the scenes, experiencing more by moving around in or doing various things to what you find in the Answer Space, and observing and describing the results.
- By *Feature-Questioning*—asking other objects or features in the experience, "Why are you here in this experience, what role do you play in this answer?", then observing and describing how the scene changes or what else happens in response.
- Likewise, by pursuing the *Clarification Question*—asking your inner resources to help you understand the answer by showing you the same answer to the same question in an entirely different scene. Usually, three different scenes that display the same answer are enough to let you infer the meaning from their common elements.
- Among the images, items that don't fit with the rest of the story, or items that in some other way oddly attract your attention, are often a key. These are your inner mind's way of highlighting where significance might be found. Were there any such special or odd features in any of your Image-Streams?
- *The Humorous Analyst*. Pose as one of the great students of human symbolism and metaphor—Sigmund Freud, Karl Jung, or Milton Erickson—and playfully ascribe the images you've

- had to your client. Speculate or brainstorm the possible meanings of these images using your professional acumen.
- By replaying some of the images in your mind's eye from your Image-Stream. Then, in the context of what these images may or may not represent, quickly describe in writing (*Freenote*) whatever comes to mind for 15-20 minutes.
- By choosing and trying another method for finding your answer or problem solution.

There may be times when the images you get as your answer or solution are absolute beauty and art. In these cases, the overwhelming beauty may obscure the answer to your question.

Such occurrences are unlikely in your early Image-Streaming experiences. If they do happen, just appreciate the beauty, even while seeking the meaning.

Besides the practical benefits of obtaining specific answers to specific questions and issues, the effect of seeking meaning in your images is great for stimulating your brain, as you iterate back and forth between conceptual understanding and your subtle ranges of perception.

Follow-up Questions

If you still have not understood the answer, describe the changes that occur in your scene or impressions when you ask such questions as:

- How can I make sure that I have the correct understanding of my answer here?
- How can I validate this answer?
- What else should I know about this situation?
- How best can I turn this answer into useful action?
- What's the first step in implementing this answer?
- What is the best thing for me to ask at this time, and the best answer to it?

Creative Problem-Solving

Most approaches to creative problem-solving teach that one has to invest 90% or more of one's total effort in finding the right question to ask about a situation. Yet, your inner resources already know the most cogent question to ask about a given situation. So asking that last question directly saves you considerable time and effort.

Other Triggers

In future exercises you can vary your initial imagery (the garden) and the screening device (the wall) as you prefer. There are many ways to get a running start in describing scenery in preparation for entering your Answer Space. Any of these can serve as a neutral starting point for *Over the Wall* so you don't start right on top of your problem. Any screening device that blocks your view of the Answer Space will do. Instead of physical screening devices, you could use the sheer rush and speed of your description to sweep you to where the answer is on display.

With all of these variants, you must still pose some problem or question that you truly, even passionately, desire to answer. Write it down as with the garden/wall experience. Then set the whole issue aside and go into any pleasant, non-confronting place, such as the beach, a forest, an amusement park, whatever place you choose, as long as you block some location from view. That location is your Answer Space and can be separated by any object, such as a wall, a door, or a closed window blind, by distance, or by time.

You can use any device that you desire to get from here to your Answer Space. You can use a car, a plane, or an elevator, as long as you conceal your Answer Space from your initial neutral area and use speed or surprise to enter your Answer Space to bypass your internal editor. You can even imagine becoming a dry leaf or dandelion fluff that is being swept up by the wind, racing along enormous landscapes to wherever the wind takes you.

Use whatever location or screening device you desire. Continue to describe faster than your editor can keep up with. Your inner visions will carry you into surprising new perceptions beyond your editor's initial acceptance space.

Image-Streaming

You can easily think of hundreds of devices for triggering a flow of images and experiences without directing the images themselves. These are often especially attractive experiences, and it would be easy to run these without actually solving issues and problems. However, with each of these triggers, do:

- Select and write down a significant question or problem beforehand so that the experience can show you its solution.
- Remember during the experience to orient on one particular feature and ask it why it's there in that context. Then watch and describe what changes occur in the scene in response to the question.
- Ask to be shown another scene that shows you exactly the same answer to the same question, but in an entirely different way.
- Use questions to validate your answer and to develop specific actions. When you don't know what you should be asking, ask what it is you should be asking and its best answer. Ask what more you need to know about that context.

This isn't just an exercise. This is your opportunity to take up real issues and problems and solve them. If in doubt as to what problem to set out to solve, ask your visual thinking faculties what problem you should solve now!

The Answer Space can also be a place for Image-Streaming if you choose to go over the wall without a specific problem in mind. With slight modifications, the Answer Space can be made to reveal inventions, new scientific discoveries, new works of art or art forms, and even new methods for solving problems!

Finding Problems

Every day of our lives we are faced with numerous problems to be resolved, decisions to be made, and questions to be answered. Often, we simply respond to the situation using our readily available, preprogrammed responses that have been established through years of experiences. Other times, we find it difficult to provide an immediate

Creative Problem-Solving

response, perhaps due to insufficient conscious information or conflicting ideas. Although Image-Streaming may be of value for moving beyond your preprogrammed responses in ordinary cases, it is found to be of significant value when dealing with intractable problems..

To gain experience with Image-Streaming and problem-solving, you need to identify a situation to be explored that requires a response for evaluation and validation. Often, when asked on the spot, people have difficulty identifying such a situation. To help you identify your own personal list of recent issues, try the following process.

Sit down and describe in writing, as quickly as possible, one specific day in your life, or re-create a typical day. In the process of this description, look for problems, questions, or decisions that came up and that you left unresolved.

Or review some aspect of your life, such as your personal relationships, your job, or your hobbies, and look for opportunities to resolve open issues or gain more insight. Place an asterisk in your text next to any issue that you identify and want to pursue later.

You will find that you can easily identify situations that you have left unresolved or unanswered and that need to be pursued. From your notes, make a list of problems, questions, or decisions that you need to address. These can be used as the bases for your Image-Streaming experience or for some specific problem-solving exercises. These are the best types of issues to address, since they are very specific to you and you have an emotional link with each one.

Another approach is to review printed material for ideas. A good source for problems can be found by reviewing a local newspaper or magazine. Your daily newspaper can provide ideas on a wide range of topics.

If you are looking to be innovative in your field of expertise or product design, review the printed matter available in your field. Or look around the room and pick an object that you want to improve. Global problems can often be found by reviewing national or international newsmagazines.

The subjects listed below are provided to help you identify issues for further investigation, using your problem-solving procedures:

Image-Streaming

Personal issues:
- Career changes: new job, new assignment, new field
- Relationships: spouse, children, friends, customers, supervisor, fellow workers
- Health issues: costs, treatment, care
- Product design issues or new product ideas
- Housing needs, changes, remodeling
- Reducing your commute time or improving traffic control
- Community problems: schools, playgrounds, sports
- Personal financial issues or plans
- School, educational, or learning issues
- New ideas for your next article, presentation, book, play
- Self-knowledge, self-development
- Daily planning, what to accomplish today
- How best to present these new ideas to...?

Global issues:
- World food shortage
- World energy shortage
- Illegal immigrants
- Tax issues: collection and usage
- Terrorism, wars
- Violence in the cities
- Growing poor population
- Bigotry, discrimination issues
- Communication issues
- Adverse impact of advertisements, movies, television
- Equal rights
- Censorship: books, movies, news
- Distorted news, ideas, beliefs
- Cultural integration and separation

Creative Problem-Solving

The more personal your issue, the more likely it is that you will be emotionally involved and motivated to find an answer or meaning. In some cases, you may find it difficult to shut down your internal editor or squelcher. This resistance typically occurs with those problems where you already have a very strong opinion, such as many of the global problems listed above. You may find that your *standard* answer continues to appear even when you are looking for alternatives.

In these cases, you may consider changing your approach by using a different question, statement of the problem, or process. Other Project Renaissance processes, such as *High Thinktank* (Chapter 6) provide alternate methods to get past your internal editor or standard responses. See Appendices D and E for a list of other processes and resources available to you.

These ideas may help you identify issues for further investigation if none are immediately apparent.

Dreams

Many people have tried to address the meaning or interpretation of dreams. There must be hundreds of books available on this subject. It is our experience that everyone has their own individual code of meanings, and it is not practical to get your dreams interpreted by someone else's formula. It is also our experience that a third or more of your dreams appear to consist of brain housecleaning and do not have any special messages or metaphors embedded in them.

However, to investigate a dream that you think does have a message or metaphor in it, you can bring the dream back to life and use any of the methods described in *Getting the Meaning of Your Images* to help you interpret its meaning.

To bring a dream back to life, simply close your eyes and describe a scene from the dream. Continue until you notice that you are experiencing images in your mind's eye. Whether or not these images seem to belong to the dream, switch to describing them, as you would while Image-Streaming. Usually these will prove to be other images from the dream that you may not have remembered at first. Or, this may be another way for your inner resources to present the same

Image-Streaming

message in a manner different from those images embedded in the dream.

At this point, proceed to elicit the meaning using the methods described earlier in this chapter in *Getting the Meaning of Your Images*. These methods include, in brief:

- Further description
- Debriefing into a different medium
- *Feature-questioning*
- Searching for oddities
- *Inductive inference* (with two short Image-Streams that are asked to provide the same message but with entirely different images)
- Playing *Analyst*
- *Freenoting*—rapidly describing in writing for 15-20 minutes whatever comes to mind in the context of the dream

If you have the interest, these ideas may help you in pursuing or exploring the meaning of your dreams.

Chapter 3: Accelerated Learning

What is accelerated learning?

You have been studying and learning throughout your life. The efficiency and effectiveness that we achieve in this process is subject to how we have been taught to learn. In most cases, though, we have never been taught an efficient or effective way to learn.

The purpose of accelerated learning is to provide processes and techniques that address this failure and that enable you to improve the efficiency and effectiveness of your time spent in the learning process.

Many people are familiar with learning processes associated with memorizing facts. Many people have described and provided programs for more efficient and effective memorization of data.

The processes provided here are not intended to address this type of learning.

The processes described below address situations where you have a complex system of information and facts that need to be assimilated in a manner that provides meaningful interrelationships and knowledge.

You are going to be an expert in this field of endeavor and you need to have a basis for using this knowledge in future opportunities.

This is the step in going from someone who can repeat a list of facts on a specific subject to the expert in a specialized field who is able to apply his organized knowledge and understanding in productive and creative applications.

The processes that follow are only a sampling of the processes developed and documented by Project Renaissance. See Appendices D and E for additional methods, processes, and resources.

Image-Streaming

Instant Replay

Instant Replay is a process for obtaining more meaning or understanding from an event, such as a lecture, a meeting, or a confrontation with a worker or relative.

Although it is best done as soon as possible after the event, you can still use it to obtain extra value from an earlier event.

Perhaps something happened with another person that you would like to have a better understanding of.

Perhaps you are in school and want to get more out of your time and effort.

Perhaps you've attended a workshop that seems to have more value than already recognized.

Perhaps you are in an athletic competition and want to improve your edge.

Whatever your purpose, *Instant Replay* is so simple and basic that it proves immediately useful in a wide variety of different situations. It can provide you with a far better understanding of any event or situation than can be obtained from a video recording that you could replay over and over.

As soon as possible after an event or situation that you would like to understand more clearly, get your recorder or locate a friend. It is slightly better if this is someone who has experienced the same event, but it is not worth a delay if no one currently available was present.

This process is similar to an astronaut's debriefing upon his return from some mission. By describing every detail of the mission or event in rich detail as described below, you will surprise yourself by receiving as much as five times more insight, meaning, and understanding from the event.

As with brainstorming, the last ideas discovered tend to be more valuable than the first conventional ideas and observations.

If you try *Instant Replay* frequently, you will find that almost every event, however simple or ordinary, is surprisingly rich with unsuspected meaning, implications, and perceptions.

Instant Replay will make your ordinary life astonishingly richer. Perhaps this is how truly creative geniuses perceive things, not realizing that what they perceive is far more than the average person perceives. Perhaps they see tumultuous, fiery-red and orange sunsets while the rest of us barely notice that the sun is setting!

After building this richness in perception, you may never want to go back to your old way of unconsciously moving through each day. You may wonder why and how you could have let yourself be so unaware and deprived.

However enriching *Instant Replay* is, the first few times you try it should be on events or situations where there is a special meaning or where you believe there is more to understand than you have noticed so far. The effect of running these special cases through *Instant Replay* may motivate you to pursue this practice on even ordinary events or situation to see how they can be enriched.

Practicing *Instant Replay* for 15-30 minutes per day on whatever events you choose should enrich your perceptions noticeably within ten days. After twenty-one days of this practice, your entire life will be several times richer in both perceptions and understandings forever. This ten hours of practice seems to be a reasonably good investment to increase by several times, for one's entire life, the experiential rewards of living.

Whatever the event or situation that you replay, follow these guidelines for *Instant Replay*:

1. Relax, close your eyes, and describe the event or situation aloud.
2. Describe it to a recorder or listener. The use of an external focus will help draw out new perceptions for you.
3. Describe the event in the present tense. Describe it as if the event were happening at this very moment. Some people find this difficult, but the rewards make the effort worth it.
4. Start by describing your sensory impressions of the setting, the presenter, the participants, the activities, and your feelings and awareness, even if you feel that you are making some of it up. Dwell on this sensory detail for four to five minutes before getting into information, ideas, or meanings. You will find these latter thoughts to be far richer than they would have been otherwise.

Image-Streaming

    5. Describe in such detail that you literally force anyone who is listening to fully experience the event you are describing. Re-create its reality through the richness of your description.
    6. From the start, make sure your eyes are closed. That way you will find yourself looking at what you are describing and beyond!
    7. Once you become aware of having mental images, they may soon change in some unexpected, even bizarre way, or be replaced by new images.

    These new images are a reflexive response from the beyond-conscious regions of your mind. This symbolic response is providing you with a vital point that you need to become conscious of. Here is the true beginning of visual thinking. Keep on describing, but switch to describing these changing or new images, and you will soon discover a crucial "aha!"

If what you describe was a lecture or workshop, you may discover more significant insights and effects than the lecturer or teacher was even aware of!

If this was a totally *free* and *open* exercise, you will certainly *capture* far more perceptions and understandings than anyone had before, including yourself.

The whole process should last between ten and thirty minutes. Your later "aha's" are usually much better than your first ones, although these "aha's" are often intertwined or dependent upon each other.

If you miss some of the points while completing this exercise, that's all right. You will still get many of the benefits.

If you are working with a listener, we suggest that you take turns and let the listener replay an event, also. What is even better is when you both replay the same event. Experiencing the *Instant Replay* process from the aspect of both speaker and listener is well worthwhile.

A variation on the *Instant Replay* process is provided below. This variation moves you more from an observer to a participant.

Experiment with this version while revisiting some workshop, lecture, or other event.

1. Relax, close your eyes, and start describing the event as you would have in *Instant Replay* until images come alive in your mind's eye.
2. Once the images come alive, imagine walking around behind the presenter while continuing to describe your impressions. Then, step forward into the presenter's body, bringing your eyes to where his or her eyes are, your ears to where his or her ears are, and so forth.
3. Now, quickly bring yourself to the point where you've become the presenter. Gaze out on the audience through the eyes of the presenter. Listen to the sounds through the ears of the presenter. Experience this whole event through and with the mind and body of the presenter, using his or her senses, thoughts, memories, and feelings.
4. Describe the differences between what you perceive now and what you had perceived when you first started describing the event.
5. Continue exploring the presenter's expertise even beyond what was presented during the event. Afterwards, you will have fun validating what you have discovered from this experience.

This head-to-head technique enables you to make just about anyone into an invaluable teacher for you.

Because these remarkably expanded perceptual resources are so extraordinarily sensitive, you may be astonished at the insights you discover from this experience. Recognize that, despite the feelings of certainty that *may* accompany such an experience, all human perceptions and interpretations of the world differ from reality to some degree. If you contemplate an important action based upon one of these experiences, please validate the experience to the degree that it is important. You owe yourself the assurance of validating your important new perceptions and insights.

Image-Streaming

This same head-to-head technique can also serve as a convenient tool for mutual understanding and for assimilating perceptions across cultural and ethnic boundaries. Create your own experiments and discover your own special uses. For additional information and methods similar to this process, see the Project Renaissance publications on *Borrowed Genius*[8].

Predictive Imagery

Predictive Imagery is a fascinating demonstration of *a priori* knowledge that the Socratics believed everyone had. It's an extraordinary phenomenon as easily demonstrated and explained as *Image-Streaming*. The images are not predictive in terms of predicting the future, but of predicting the contents of a book, a lecture, or an entire course and subject, previously unknown to an individual.

In this section, we will focus on applying the principle of *Predictive Imagery* to reducing the time it takes you to read a book, monograph, or other heavy assignment and increasing the intellectual value or understanding you gain from such readings.

You will learn how to reduce your reading time by two-thirds and triple your comprehension during the activity.

This combination produces a nine-fold improvement, whether you are a student wrestling with assignments or a professional trying to keep up with the literature in your own field.

Some years ago, while Win was teaching in Stockholm, he was invited to dinner at the home of his Swedish publisher. During this very pleasant occasion, the publisher's daughter complained that, after considerable effort, she couldn't make heads or tails of a major reading assignment she had been given in school. Was there any way Win could help her? This was a girl who normally was at or near the top of

---

[8] See the Project Renaissance website, www.winwenger.com/borrow1.htm, and also one of the volumes in this Core Books series.

Accelerated Learning

her class, but this time she was stymied. Having ascertained that she was able to Image-Stream, Win got her to try a little experiment.

"Ask your Image-Stream to show you an image that will make everything in your reading assignment come together and make immediate sense to you.... What do you see?" She saw a white bird along with some other details. Win suggested that she "hang that picture on the back wall of her mind" and return to the reading assignment. A short time later, she burst back into the dining room all excited because everything in that assignment *did* come together for her and made immediate sense!

For Win, this experiment had stopped being an experiment many years before and dozens of individuals ago. But it was nice to have this example happen in front of others. In this particular instance, Win never did find out the meaning of the white bird image. However, the image fulfilled the necessary function in this context.

To apply this process, simply follow these two simple steps to increase your speed of reading and understanding of material where intellectual or aesthetic understanding is needed:
1. Just before reading a chapter, article or complete text, orient yourself to what you're about to do. Ask your Image-Stream to show you an image that will somehow make everything in this reading assignment come together for you and make immediate sense.
2. Whatever the image, describe and record the details of it. Keep the image in the back of your mind and start your reading assignment.

Watch what happens! You will discover, with some amazement, that everything in that reading assignment comes together and makes sense to you in less than a third of the time that it would ordinarily have taken you! Your understanding will be many times greater than you would have otherwise experienced.

Predictive Imagery seems to provide a kind of intellectual coat rack on which you can hang the various understandings as you are reading. They are hung where you can easily pluck them for retrieval!

57

Although this is true, there seems to be more to this experience than simply establishing a coat rack to hang your understandings on.

Can you accomplish the same thing using an arbitrarily selected image? If so, you'd get the same results by arbitrarily picking some picture out of a magazine or newspaper and letting it play that role. Although this has not been formally measured, our experience has indicated that the results of using an arbitrary picture simply do not compare with those where your Image-Stream creates an image that is specific to the particular reading assignment.

As demonstrated by the Socratic Method, you have within you much more information and understanding than you are consciously aware of. The *Predictive Imagery* process provides you with the ability in some way to predict the contents of a particular reading assignment before you start it. The resultant image is uniquely suited to meshing the concepts from your reading assignment with your conscious understanding.

The *Predictive Imagery* accelerated learning method also applies to obtuse lectures or other hard-to-follow presentations. Creating your images just prior to attending the lecture will provide you with the same effect as using the process in your reading assignments. You can apply the same process to an entire course of study. Specific details for applying *Predictive Imagery* in other applications can be found in other Project Renaissance materials (see Appendices D and E).

What Did I Leave Out?

Here is another simple learning improvement method that has many uses outside of the learning environment, as well.

Use this process upon completion of an essay, a written assignment, planning your presentation, or whatever lengthy, involved task or creative project you are completing. When you are ready, ask your Image-Stream to show you a picture of what you've inadvertently left out of your project that you should have included! Or, ask what the most important aspect of the project is that you should enhance or highlight!

Chances are, you will be shown a significant point that you should include! If you don't immediately understand what your image means, thank your inner resources and ask them to show you another, entirely different picture of the same fact or idea. What's the same in these otherwise very different images? If you answer this question after examining two or three such images, you should recognize the key fact or idea.

Cognitive Structural Enhancement

Jean Piaget was a Swiss biologist who is known as the founder of cognitive psychology.

While closely observing infants and young children, Piaget found that our powers of understanding grow from a sequence of more basic experiences. He found that our ability to understand rests upon more basic understandings and that these, in turn, rest upon even more basic sensory experiences.

As babies, we needed to experience a lot of things to learn what we take for granted today. For instance, playing peek-a-boo enables a baby to discover whether the existence of things depends upon its looking at them or not. This seems awfully elementary, and it is. Piaget called this phenomenon the "principle of conservation." This principle helps build the basis from which we could understand other concepts.

As young children, we would play with objects. As we did, we learned about the concept of volume by pouring fluid into differently shaped containers. This activity led us to realize that the volume of the fluid and the volume of the container are related to the quantity of liquid that a container can hold.

We needed to understand this "principle of constancy" in order to build the structure in our mind to understand that actions are reversible. You can pour water from one container into another and then pour it back.

We also needed play to understand that not all actions are reversible; for example, pouring water on the ground is not reversible.

Image-Streaming

Gaps in the Structure of Our Understanding

If we missed some of these basic experiences in our life, then we may have some gaps in our structure of understanding.

These gaps could make it harder for us to understand what's going on around us today. For instance, if we never learned through first-hand experience that the volume of the water stays the same regardless of the shape of the container, we would have eventually learned this information from someone else.

If such a gap happened along our path of development, we may never really understand how some things are reversible and some things are not. That's quite a shortfall in our understanding, even if it does only apply to a small degree!

Actually, we *all* have gaps in our structure of basic understandings. These ideas were simply taught to us as facts. It would have been better if we had discovered these ideas through our own sensory experience.

A Nice Little Dilemma

The more basic the principle, the farther away it is from our current conscious attention. Yet the more basic the principle, the more it applies to nearly everything. So the more basic the gap, the more often we experience situations in which our understanding is weakened and the greater its negative effect on our lives. In addition, it will be that much harder for us to track down the missing parts through our conscious memory.

If we were to repair such a gap, it would make a positive difference throughout our life. We now suggest that you can repair these gaps in your understanding by following the simple *Cognitive Structural Enhancement* procedure described below.

To Repair Those Gaps and Strengthen Your Structure of Understanding

The purpose of these instructions is to help you discover one of your key gaps, to repair that gap, and ultimately to strengthen your powers of understanding for all matters dependent upon this basic understanding. Even with such a little explanation, your beyond-

Accelerated Learning

conscious mind already knows and has selected for you one of these critical gap points in your development.

If possible, have a friend read the following instructions to you while you do what is asked. If no one is available, you can record these instructions with suitable pauses for playback. During playback, describe your images to another recorder. With someone leading you or with these instructions being cued to you, you will more fully enter the experience with your eyes closed.

Arrange a place so that you can provide your full attention to the experience for at least one half-hour or so.

Cognitive Structural Enhancement Instructions

1. Let your Image-Stream take you back to some key point early in your intellectual development...some point way back in your life... Drift back to some early point in your life... Without trying to recall events, without trying to remember early memories, just let your Image-Stream open on a key point of your early development. Whether or not it seems to fit, just let any impression or image unfold for you. Describe your images in rich sensory detail to the listener. *[Allow 3-4 minutes for this description.]*

2. Now, imagine the most effective and appropriate experience that could have best enriched your understanding at that key point instead of what did happen... Whatever image comes to you, build upon it by using all of your senses in the experience. Continue describing your experience... *[Allow 4 to 8 minutes for further description.]*

3. Excellent. Now come forward a little in time to some other point in your life, a little more recently in your past, a point in your life where the new understanding you've just been exploring would have made a difference. Then let's explore that difference. First, let your Image-Stream come to that more recent point of past experience. Whatever images come before you, let things unfold with this new basic

Image-Streaming

understanding and appreciation as part of it... Let your Image-Stream move you forward in time, from that very early experience in your life, to other key points of development that followed directly from such a basic area of understanding. What was a later point in your life where the key understanding from this early experience would have made a lot of difference... Let your images take you to that later point of time in your life where having that earlier understanding would have made a difference to you. Continue to describe whatever images come now... *[Allow 4 to 7 minutes for describing.]*

4. Good. Let your Image-Streaming move forward to a later point in your life before the present moment. This later point is also a moment where that early understanding would have made quite some difference to you. Continue describing whatever images come now... *[Allow 3½ to 7 minutes for such describing.]*

 [Optionally, if this experience is going very well and productively, continue with:] Let your Image-Stream move you further forward in time from there, along your life's development between then and this present moment in time... Go to one or several more such points in your life experience where having that very basic understanding would somehow have made a very big difference to you. Please describe each of these experiences to me... *[Allow maybe 3-6 minutes for each such experience to be described.]*

5. There is always something more or something new to discover that can enhance your wonderful powers of understanding even further. Your next experience with this process can be different. You may find and repair some other gap in your structure of understanding, as you build your ever-burgeoning powers of understanding, as everything around you and everything in your life takes on new dimensions of meaning.

 For now, let's come back fully to the present moment in time and space.... Coming fully alert, remarkably refreshed and feeling clear, yawning and stretching, coming fully alert and *feeling terrific*!

6. Now, please take 10 or 15 minutes more to describe to your listener, *and* to a notepad, some of the specific improvements that you feel this particular episode or set of experiences has made in your present-day understanding and perception.

Mark off three days on your calendar. Select a specific time when you take out your recorder or notepad.

Review any other differences you have noticed since the foregoing experience.

Have you noticed any changes in your understandings or in your life? In what ways have various sectors of your life become richer?

Clear understanding makes our perceptions of *everything* so much richer and more rewarding. This simple half-hour procedure is a direct way to build our understanding and our ability *to* understand.

This repair for your track of development is only *one* of the many uses of Image-Streaming.

Chapter 4: Image-Streaming for Children

Help a Young Child to Flower

Some of you may be wondering how you can use Image-Streaming with young children and what its advantages might be. For young children it appears to be even more helpful and powerful than for adults. Included here are two processes that you can use for young children through 11 years of age and one for older children, aged 7 to 12 years. You can personally witness the impact of Image-Streaming in a young child. In the days following a child's Image-Streaming experience, you will find extraordinary improvements in the child's general joy of life, not merely his quality of perception and insight.

To teach a young child Image-Streaming, become a little smooth at Image-Streaming yourself. This process will prepare you to demonstrate the procedure for your child. You can introduce this simple procedure as soon as a child is able to use language.

Once you are smooth with your own Image-Streaming and you feel confident that you can provide a realistic demonstration, follow these instructions:

1. Start by saying something like, "John (or Mary), I think that even when we are awake, we still have dreams going on somewhere inside of us. Let's see, when I close my eyes and look to see what's going on there, I see..."

2. Now describe your Image-Stream as a demonstration for the child. For example, you might state:

    "Two green bushes, must be springtime because most of the leaves are dark green but some leaves are smaller and almost golden toward the tips of the branches — Two entirely different sets of leaves on the same bush — The grass is just starting to turn green, still a lot of gray and brown there — I see a moss-covered brick sidewalk in front of the bushes..."

3. Next, start the child Image-Streaming by stating something such as, "OK, for fun, John (or Mary), when you close your eyes, tell me what you see there..."

If need be, *play the game* with another adult or an older child to model the process. Then let the young child join in. Because of a shorter attention span and simpler vocabulary, a young child responds to this approach far better than to the lengthier steps used to describe the process for an adult.

Often, a very young child will just name objects instead of describing them. Although this is an important start, you want to get the child to describe things. This is true whether things are actually visualized, made up, or present in the here and now and objectively described. The more sensorily rich and detailed the description, the sooner and stronger the resulting brain and language develop. When Image-Streaming with eyes closed, the child's innate visual thinking abilities will come back sooner and continue to become stronger.

To encourage actual description instead of the mere naming of things, make a game of it. Ask an older child or another adult to demonstrate the descriptive process until the young child joins in. If need be, walk around the house and demonstrate that you can make richly detailed descriptions of very ordinary objects and situations. Even without visualizing, this is an invaluable way to develop the left brain of the child with the child's entire perceiving and reasoning process.

In teaching young children how to Image-Stream, it's easier with older children who have better developed vocabularies; but its effects are more powerful and immediately visible in younger children.

The benefits of Image-Streaming appear to be permanent. It can be quite rewarding to view the effects on children and to know you had something to do with enriching a child's development.

Practical Problem-Solving for Children

With somewhat older children, ages 4-11, here is a simple way to extend Image-Streaming. This procedure will equip the child to cope effectively with many things that other children are helpless against. Once some problem, question or difficulty has been identified, tell the child:

1. "Imagine a door. Something like a dream is on the far side of that door. That dream may tell you a clever and effective solution to this problem, or at least one that works."

2. "Dreams being what they are, the answer may not be in words, but somehow in what is shown to you. Maybe some of what is shown to you will surprise you, or seem to have nothing to do with answering the problem. But when we look at it more closely, maybe we'll find somehow that the answer is in there somewhere."

3. "Let's be on this side of the closed door first. Start by telling me everything about the door when we see it from this side. Tell me everything about the door that you're looking at..."

4. "When you're ready, open your door suddenly and tell me what you see there on the other side of it..."

If the child has had some Image-Streaming experience, he or she should be ready to get intelligible answers from beyond the door. You may need to make a game once or twice of seeing and telling what's beyond the door before it is used with a problem or difficulty.

If the actual answer is not readily apparent, have the child go through another door seeking an answer to the same problem. But this time, ask for an entirely different scene that somehow provides the same answer. If you have enough descriptive detail from both scenes, some details or aspects will overlap. What you find that is the same when everything else is different is the core to the actual answer. Looking for the similarities and differences may be better for the child's mental development than any particular answer might be. Please refrain from interpreting for your child or getting between your child and access to his/her own inner resources. You can ask slightly leading questions, but let the child discover the answer, even if it takes awhile. You'll be so very glad you did.

The World Next Door

The World Next Door is an improved learning experience for children ages 7 to 12.

Whether a teacher, parent, grandparent, aunt or uncle, you may have felt some concern at what's been happening to children that you care about. These children may be in very good learning programs, but you still would like to do something to help them along. Therefore, we are providing you with an additional tool that can make a positive, meaningful difference. *The World Next Door* strongly enables your children to learn far more effectively and pleasantly. It goes well beyond the tools provided above.

Although it can be used with a single child, the following procedure has been prepared for use with a classroom of children who are arranged to sit and talk together in pairs.

Before the exercise is started, identify one child in each pair as the first speaker during each break in the description. They can alternate as the first speaker during the *buzz* sessions. If you want to use this procedure with an individual child, simply replace "partner" with "tell me" in the instructions.

Special instructions are provided in brackets and are not to be read aloud. They are provided to guide you as you read through the steps to the class or child.

The entire procedure should take 20-35 minutes. Maintain a steady pace throughout the process. If you are leading a classroom, find a chime or other instrument that you can use to provide an agreeable *ting*. If you are working with just one child, a chime is optional.

When you are ready, read aloud the following procedure, creating a little make-believe adventure in better learning.

Image-Streaming

1. "Imagine there's a world next door that's very like our world, but a little different. Imagine that if you look in a mirror just right, you can see into that world."

2. "Imagine that in that world next door lives someone that's very much like you. In a way that someone is you, a version of you that is part of and living in the world next door. Maybe the version of you in the mirror is just a little older than you are, and, is very good at something you aren't yet very good at."

3. "Maybe we can find out all sorts of things in that world next door. The world that's like ours, but different. A world that is next door to us, but one where you may have to look in the mirror in a special way to see. Maybe we can find out from that version of you who lives next door, how they got so good at something that you aren't yet good at, but would like to be."

4. "This is a make-believe world. But, maybe we can discover useful things from it and from the version of you who lives there. So what would you like to be good at, that you aren't yet good at? Please turn to your partner, and, tell each other what you would like to be good at, and why you would like to be good at it."
   [Allow 1-2 minutes for this discussion by the children (buzz session). At the end of this time, strike your chime once gently, pause for about 30 seconds, then strike the chime gently three times and say:]

5. "Now imagine there is a big, full-length mirror in front of you and you are looking into it. Imagine that somehow you've hit upon the right way to look into the mirror so you can see that world next door. From here, that world looks pretty much the same as ours does here, but, maybe you can spot a few differences. Looking back at you in the mirror is that other version of you. This other version of you looks just like you,

only maybe a little bit older, and maybe different in one or two other ways that you'll notice sooner or later."

6. "Looking in the mirror at this version of you, tell your partner what you see in as much detail as possible. Use lots of adjectives to describe what you are seeing. Then, let your partner tell you what they see when looking into their own mirror."
[Allow the discussion between the children to continue for 2-3 minutes (buzz session). Strike the chime once gently, pause for about 30 seconds, then chime gently three more times and say:]

7. "Now imagine or make-believe that the edges of the mirror are looking a little funny, almost as if they were softening or melting. Imagine reaching out to touch the mirror. Instead of touching the mirror, your hand passes through the mirror with a little tingling feeling in your hand."

8. "Should you go through the mirror? Maybe! Raise an eyebrow to your other version to ask if it's all right with him or her. Ask if you can come over for five minutes by holding up your hand and spreading your five fingers. If your other version nods or smiles back at you, then it's O.K. You're welcome to visit."

9. "When you're ready, step through the mirror. Maybe there's a light tingling sensation as you step through the mirror into this world-next-door. When you are through, look around. Walk around a bit to see more of what's there. Maybe everything is the same as back here, maybe some things are different. Because this is make-believe, you can be over there while still talking with your partner at the same time. Tell your partner what you're seeing and let your partner tell you what they see. As you look and walk around in the world-next-door, tell your partner every detail of what you see there."

Image-Streaming

[Buzz for 2-3 minutes. Strike the chime once gently, pause for about 30 seconds, then strike the chime gently three more times and say:]

10. "You would now like to see the thing that your other version in the mirror is really good at doing. Go with your other version to where they can show you what it's like to be so very, very good at this thing you'd like to be good at too. Watch as closely as you can as they perform this thing. Describe every detail of what you're seeing there to your partner back here. Also, let your partner back here tell you their experience. Describe every detail of what you can see this other version of yourself do so very well. If you notice and tell enough details of what you're seeing this other version do and they are doing it, you may get a little of the feel of how that works. The more you can notice and describe, the better the chances are that you can get the hang of this thing and be able to do it a little better yourself. How is this other version of you doing this thing so very well? Notice everything you can about that and describe it to your partner."

[Buzz session for 2-3 minutes. If you want to end the exercise at this point, go to step 11. If you want to run more powerful versions of this exercise, continue with either Step 10A or 10B. This depends upon how powerful you want to make this learning experience. Step 10A is somewhat more powerful while Step 10B is even more so. Either step can be followed prior to Step 11. Strike the chime once gently, pause for about 30 seconds, then strike the chime gently three more times and proceed with Step 10A, 10B, or 11 saying:]

Optional Step 10A: "Now you can also ask the other version of you questions about what you've seen or questions about any other things. You can ask one, two, or three questions. You get only three questions on this round. When you ask your question, speak softly while asking loudly in your mind. Watch and listen carefully to see what your answer might be. Maybe the picture will change in response to your question and that will somehow be your answer. Or, your other version may point to something as the answer. If you listen intently, you may hear what your other version answers. Sometimes the answer may take some time to figure out, so report what you are observing. If needed, we can figure out what the answer is later, but at least we'll have it. Now, ask your first question. Watch as closely as possible what happens and describe what you observe."

[Buzz session for 2-5 minutes. Strike the chime once gently, pause for about 30 seconds, and then strike it gently three more times and proceed with Step 11 saying:]

Optional Step 10B: "Now, imagine that you move so that you are standing at an arm's-length behind that other version of you in the mirror. In this make-believe adventure, just walk forward into this other version of you. Bring your eyes to where his or her eyes are so that you are now looking through and with the eyes of this other version of you. Bring your ears to where his or her ears are so that you can listen to the sounds of this world-next-door through and with the ears of your other version. Bring all of yourself, for just a minute or so, to be this other version of you. From here, do more of what this other version of you is good at doing. Study how it looks and feels to be this other version of you doing this thing so well. Report to your partner everything you observe starting now."

[Buzz for 2-3 minutes. Strike the chime once gently, pause for about 30 seconds, and then strike it gently three more times and say:]

"Now, step forward out of your other version. You can hardly wait to get back to your own world to see how much better you are at this thing. You remember the feel and pattern of what this other version was doing so well. You carry this back with you to do that thing a little bit better. Thank the other version of you for their assistance. Feel the warm thanks coming back to you. This was such a neat way to share an experience."

Image-Streaming

11. "When you look back at the opening that you came through to get to the world next door, you can see us back here. It's time now. You don't want to wear out your welcome, so step back through that opening to rejoin us back here."

12. "Look backward into that world-next-door and perhaps you can see the other version of you waving good-bye. Let the opening turn back into a mirror again. Look at just your own mirror image once more. Now send away the mirror. Put away the make-believe for now and be fully here, in this room. Let's find out what each other saw over there."

This scripted experience for improved learning is only one of many possible children's versions of procedures for improved learning, creative problem-solving, and enhanced intelligence based upon the processes developed by Project Renaissance. This procedure is now available from Nightingale-Conant in their audio program, *Brain Boosters—20 Minutes a Day to a More Powerful Intelligence.*

Additional information and processes similar to *The World Next Door* can also be found in Project Renaissance publications on *Borrowed Genius.*[9]

Let your children be among the ones to benefit from these processes. We hope that all children have the opportunity to reach their full potential. Explore using these processes with your children and their friends whenever you have the opportunity.

---

[9] Project Renaissance website, www.winwenger.com/borrow1.htm and also one of the volumes in this Core Books series.

Chapter 5: Image-Streaming for Groups

Once you've learned and practiced Image-Streaming for yourself, you can share the rewards of this activity with as many people as you like. You can teach any-sized groups, even hundreds at a time if you have the opportunity. What follows is a step-by-step description of how to facilitate this worthwhile activity.

After making sure that everyone in your group is available for the next thirty minutes without interruption, obtain an agreement that no one will strand his or her partner once the process has begun.

Introduce the sound of a chime or water-glass as an agreed-upon signal to pause in talking so additional instructions can be heard when the time comes. The chime will be struck once as notice to wrap up your current activities. The chime will be struck three times to indicate that everyone's full attention should immediately be given to the leader.

To introduce this system to the group, you might say, "The chime will be struck once as a signal that you should complete your talking shortly. When the chime is struck three times, you should immediately stop whatever you are doing and provide your attention to receive further instructions."

After you provide a brief explanation to your group, demonstrate Image-Streaming for thirty seconds to the group. Then continue with:

Image-Streaming for Groups Script

1. Say something like, "Now each of you, please close your eyes, and as soon as you get images, different from mine, hold up your hand and keep it up. Thank you." As the first few hands go up, say in a low but audible voice, "Good! Thank you! If more than half of us... Good. Very Good..." In less than 90 seconds you should find a majority of hands raised.

Image-Streaming

2. Once you have a majority with hands raised, state, "Thank you! Excellent, please keep your hands up. We are now going to form pairs. Please, everyone who didn't get an image of some sort, who didn't get their hand up, please select a partner whose hand is raised. Please keep those hands up! Now, finish forming your new pairs. Is everyone partnered with some one else? At least one member of each pair should have had images and raised their hand? Thank you!"

3. When everyone is settled into pairs, simply say: "Thank you! Those of you who got images before, those of you who raised their hands, continue pursuing more images now. This time describe them in rich detail to your partner while you are observing them. Please, only one person speaking in each pair...."

4. Every pair should have a member Image-Streaming. You might want to walk around to make sure everyone is Image-Streaming and not having difficulties. Don't be too quick to intervene.
   Make sure no one is talking about something else instead of doing the process. Once it's clear that everyone is in process, you can help the energies of the room by doing a little quiet semi-Image-Streaming of your own or, if your audience was odd-numbered, work with the spare member.

5. After five to ten minutes, gently sound the chime and quietly say, "As easily as that! Now reverse roles. The Image-Streamer becomes the new listener and the old listener becomes the new Image-Streamer. New Image-Streamers, please look at your images and describe them in rich detail to your partner, beginning now...."

6. Having witnessed the initial demonstration of Image-Streaming, observing their partner's Image-Streaming, and seeing it happen all around, it's the most natural thing in the

Image-Streaming for Groups

world for any previously non-imaging participants to slip into their own images and start describing them. You should walk around to make sure no one needs further help or encouragement.

7. After the new Image-Streamers have had six to ten minutes of Image-Streaming, gently sound the chime and say, "Carrying on, let's switch activities. The current Image-Streamer should now become the new listener, and the current listener now becomes the new Image-Streamer. All of you should now have your own images. .... Now, when the speaker pauses for a breath, the other partner should step in and start describing. When the current speaker pauses for breath, switch once more, the current listeners step in and describe more of their own ongoing Image-Stream. Continue...."

8. Stroll among your participants, as before, mainly for an encouragement, since everyone should have had some Image-Streaming experience. You can let this phase go anywhere from five to fifteen minutes. The longer they are in process, the greater the benefits. But you don't want things to get drowsy, humdrum or restless, so at some opportune lull, gently sound the chime, saying something like, "Complete your Image-Streaming. Gently return fully alert with refreshed awareness to the here and now.... Notice how clear everything seems as you come fully alert, refreshed, and feeling good."

It's a good idea to switch to another partner and debrief to the new partner, reviewing everything that has been experienced in a condensed two- to three-minute period for each one.

If the group is continuing into other activities, those activities will go more easily and more effectively for having had this experience. That's why so many programs have begun to include Image-Streaming with what they are doing.

Since 1988, thousands of people have been taught with this simple method. There have not been any cases where the majority of the members failed to get their hands up after the first demonstration.

Image-Streaming

Back-up Procedures

Although the above procedure is simple and preferred, a variation of it is available for use as a backup approach if, for some reason, the above procedure is not successful. In this approach, we use the *Helper Techniques* cited in Chapter 1, page 18, in the section titled, *Prompting Techniques to Start Your Image-Stream*. See more in Appendix C.

To use the *Helper* variation, simply assign a Spotter to the person having difficulty starting their Image-Stream. If you prefer, have all pairs in the group participate in this activity together.

Instruct the Image-Streamer not to look for images, just to pick up on them when they come and report them in detail. He or she should simply focus on making their breathing as luxurious, smooth, and continuous as possible, with no pauses between breathing in and breathing out.

The Spotter, meanwhile, looks for pauses in the Image-Streamer's breathing, since we tend to hold our breath when giving attention to a stimulus. The Spotter should also look for movement in the Image-Streamer's eyes under the closed eyelids.

If the Spotter sees either, gently but quickly ask, "What was in your awareness just then?" This helps alert the Image-Streamer to the fact that they were seeing a tree branch, and on that tree branch was a...

Instruct the Spotter not to interrupt once the flow of description is going. Question the Image-Streamer only if the flow is stopping. The Spotter is there to encourage the flow from the Image-Streamer as a listener with minimum intervention.

Start this variation using the partner who has obtained images as the Image-Streamer speaking first. After five to ten minutes, reverse the roles. By this time, the initial non-imagers have had Image-Streaming demonstrated for them several times, and they will most likely skip right into it. If not, the Spotter should proceed as described in the previous paragraph. Then continue following the standard group instructions given above.

Another alternative to help a group of people along includes a little adventure describing *after-images*, such as those produced by a camera flash. This is concrete, specific, and it's easy for people to get involved. It has them looking toward the origin of their Image-Streams. Once they start into the descriptive process with the after-images, the descriptive process will not seem so strange to them when they start Image-Streaming.

This after-image technique is especially useful when attempting to teach people to set aside their own stock knowledge, make their own observations, and come to their own conclusions.

After-image is very useful in this case, since everyone assumes that the afterimages will disappear in just a few minutes. But experience has shown that the after-image can continue for hours if reinforced through focused description.

Workshops

During workshops, when you are actively describing your images with a partner and alternating descriptive experiences, it is very easy to be influenced in your description by what your partner or other people in the workshop are describing.

We encourage people to stay with their own imagery. Just be present with your partner as someone to describe their imagery to. It is easy for you and your partner to enter each other's experiences, reacting to features in the other's experience.

On occasion, this is seen to happen with someone else across the room, seemingly out of hearing. No matter what the cause of this response, we encourage people to follow their own images, since they are receiving messages in their own symbolic code.

Keeping their own images also makes for more accurate messages and subsequent self-interpretation. Each person's inner imagery and symbolism has been differentiated by a lifetime of experience from that of the partner. A bridge or a flagpole in someone's Image-Stream may not have the same meaning as a bridge or flagpole in another's Image-Stream.

There is a cautionary tale about the patient who had a problem, went to visit his psychiatrist, had the problem interpreted, and came out with two problems. It's much better for Image-Streaming if participants interpret only their own imagery. Otherwise, even if the

Image-Streaming

interpretation happens to be right, the interpreter stands between the person and their access to their own inner resources. This access may be more valuable than any particular answer. One of the few rules in Image-Streaming is, "Thou shalt not interpret for thy partner, only for thyself."

Enjoy the use of this procedure in any size group, whether large or small, whenever you have the opportunity.

Chapter 6:   High Thinktank

In Chapter 3, we introduced you to the use of Image-Streaming for Creative Problem-Solving in two applications that helped you get around your internal editor. In this chapter, we will take you one step further into tackling those problems or issues about which you have a very strong emotional attachment or preference.

The more important the problem, the more likely we are to have expectations and concerns that get in the way of the fresh perceptions we need in order to find a good answer. With these types of problems, it's often much more difficult to get past the interference caused by our internal editor.

This next procedure, *High Thinktank,* is designed to give you a far more powerful approach to getting past your internal editor. *High Thinktank* can be used in group or solo applications.

For best results with *High Thinktank*, you should have logged at least an hour's worth of Image-Streaming by itself or in an application such as *Over the Wall.*

Bypassing Our Internal Editor

Our conscious mind with its language ability is an excellent tool for focusing our perceptions and magnifying them so they are out "in front" of us. On the other hand, our conscious mind is so fond of its accepted world that it is usually reluctant to take in and process input from beyond itself.

 As a result, our conscious mind is very effective when we are seeking an answer to a question from the information that we already know. The difficulty arises for questions or problems that we cannot consciously resolve with the information that we "know." Then, what we "know" often blocks the receipt of the fresh perceptions that we need for good answers. For these problems, we need to go beyond our conscious mind and bypass our internal editor.

Image-Streaming

How do we cope when the editor wants to make every answer come out the way it expects? How can we access our beyond-conscious resources and get past the editor? *High Thinktank* takes advantage of the fact that our inner faculties are much more sensitive and subtle than our conscious mind. With *High Thinktank*, we can pose questions directly to these richer faculties and get our answers back before our internal editor recognizes what is happening.

Truly Great Problems

Some questions or problems are so important that our responses were formulated a long time ago. It seems impossible to look beyond these responses for fresh or useful insights. For example, what happens when someone asks, "What is the best system of government?" In this case, you are instantly assaulted by your preconceived responses. None of this noise is very useful if you are trying to reach new and unique insights to a question or problem. Many people will accept the chatter that immediately comes to mind.

Now, to get around this situation, what if you did not consciously know the question that you were trying to answer? In this case, your internal editor wouldn't know how to filter or distort your answers. What if your subtler faculties knew the question as a result of subliminal cues, unconscious pattern-recognition, or prediction, but you did not consciously know the question? Under these conditions, perhaps you could be shown an answer that your internal editor did not corrupt. *High Thinktank* enables you to use this approach to squelching your internal editor, and, as a result, lets us deal more creatively and effectively with major issues and questions.

We now introduce you to the *High Thinktank* method for group practice, followed by a version that you can use alone. The group process goes into more detail than the instructions for solo use. Studying the group process will help you in your solo application. We have found that doing this procedure with a group of co-explorers is very effective and a lot more fun than doing it alone. Yet, even the solo version is highly powerful and effective.

Group High Thinktank

Here we take advantage of the fact that much of your brain is far more sensitive to subtle cues and clues than the "loud left-side." In this procedure, your conscious brain will not have the opportunity to know the question before your answer is established.

Please note that it is *critical* that you do not try to guess what the question is. Just look in and see or read what your answer to the question is when the time comes. Just simply let go of your expectations and "look in to your own inner mind" to see what your faculties are telling you is the answer. You want to be completely free of the bias imposed by the expectations of your left brain.

If you have a large group, subdivide it into smaller groups of four to six members. This will assure more involvement from each member and achieve better development of awareness in each person. Once the groups have been formed, proceed with the following steps in each of the groups.

1. One member of each group reviews a question that he or she has selected from a list of questions without informing any one else in the group as to which question has been selected. Alternatively, select a question from a stack of folded papers with different question on each. This slip of paper is handed around to everyone in the group but its contents are not consciously seen. If the question is being asked silently by someone in the group, a nod or light finger snap is appropriate to indicate to other members of the group that he or she has completed asking the question silently.

2. As quickly as they can, each participant identifies the image in his/her mind as the answer and reports it in a simultaneous blurt. While we are depending more on "hiding" the question

Image-Streaming

than on speed in High Thinktank, it's still valuable to get that initial response made so quickly that people don't have time to pick up on one another's cues.

—OR—

Each participant silently describes his or her own image-answer by writing or sketching it for a few moments on a sheet of paper, enough on each image to support the ongoing describing to be made of these in Step 3.

3. Form pairs within each group and develop your initial responses into brief but very descriptive Image-Streams. Get as much detail as possible in the first 1 to 3 minutes each so it's easier to compare the details in Step 4.

4. Compare your respective Image-Stream answers around the group, looking for common themes and elements.

5. *After* identifying the common themes or elements, the original asker "reveals" the formerly silent or folded-in "hidden" question.

6. Explore the relationship(s) between those common theme elements as answer, and the question asked.

7. As time permits, ask follow-up questions to clarify, verify your answers and to map out ways to implement them as appropriate. Also ask yourself or as a group, what more do I/we need to know in this context?

People will often wonder, "How can I answer the question without consciously knowing what it is?" Fortunately, that subtler, more comprehensive part of your mind (99.9999%) is more sensitive, wiser, and brighter than we think. There are more than enough subliminal clues floating around to account for how we pick up the question and obtain an answer. There is trace print-through on questions written onto folded-up slips of paper; there is body language; there is subvocalization; and there are high-order predictive inference and pattern recognition. There is a wealth of information telling us what the question is that's being asked.

As a result of this process, we can get cleaner, less distorted data from our beyond-conscious mind. It is precisely *this* that makes *High Thinktank* so remarkably accurate. It's the one format where your loud left brain won't get in the way and edit your answers to suit its expectations!

Only your own practiced use of *High Thinktank* can effectively determine for you the actual relationship between the answers gotten from your more sensitive resources and the silent or hidden questions asked.

Is this process anything more than provocative random force-fit? If it is, then you are also looking at your own ability to find effective answers to virtually any question or problem in the world!

High Thinktank When Working Alone

Accumulate six or more questions in a box (or envelope). Place each question on a separate index card or folded scrap of paper so that the words are not visible. Because you have written these, your subtler resources will know which is which. But if you randomize these questions and pick one at random, your conscious left temporal isn't likely to recognize which one is which and will most likely get out of the way of the visual data-flow coming from the rest of the brain in answer to that question.

Your objective is not to "psyche out" which question that is but simply to look at what your mind is showing you as answer to it.

On the question you thus select, get three sets of images. As in the group form with the images from other participants, the three images give you a basis for comparison. Be sure to get enough sensory detail recorded from each image that it will be easy for you to spot where the many aspects of one image match aspects of another image. Each image is rich with many meanings and messages, but each image contains some form of your main answer(s) as well. This comparison

Image-Streaming

makes the key meanings stand out above all the other messages and makes it easier for you to spot and to experience your "aha!"

Only after you've mapped out these detailed comparisons from your images should you then look at the "hidden question." Read it consciously and examine how those common elements or themes actually answer your question.

Be sure to replace the answered question with another one to keep a minimum stock of six questions at all times. This will keep you from consciously trying to guess the question. The questions should be very different from one another so that the answer to one question isn't confused with another.

Doing two to four questions per day for a few days should give you the feel for the flow coming from wider sectors of your brain.

Besides the convenience of speed, High Thinktanking appears to develop some things in the brain that not even Image-Streaming does. We don't know quite what's happening with the brain in this case, but we've seen some extraordinary abilities develop and remarkable things happen that we've not seen even with regular, sustained practice of Image-Streaming. It is clear, from those of us who have pursued the "30-Day Challenge" (see below), that these two seemingly similar procedures are integrating our brains in very different configurations, both of them in a positive manner.

Until we know more about it, we recommend some practice of both Image-Streaming and High Thinktank to encourage as wide a range as possible of neuronal and brain circuitry activation and mind development.

The 30-day Challenge

A 30-day challenge is being offered for your consideration. Your challenge is to answer at least one question every day for 30 days using the *High Thinktank* process. This effort will take little time on a daily basis but requires your dedication to succeed. If you succeed, we fully guarantee that you will experience some of the most intriguing experiences of your life while developing skills and awareness to an extent even more striking than with Image-Streaming alone.

Your 30-Day Challenge Kit

This simple kit is designed to make it easy for you to process questions using *High Thinktank*. You will need a small envelope to carry with you and whip out whenever you get a chance. Take advantage of some "in-between-time" such as:

- a pause before or after telephone calls
- just before or after you've propped your feet up in front of the TV
- a few minutes before or after lunch or dinner
- when you are riding with someone and they are driving

You probably have 20 to 30 such opportunities each day. All you need to do is to use at least one of these opportunities every day for 30 consecutive days. If you miss one, continue anyway until you reach the 30 days. Things will happen.

Within that envelope, you should carry 8 to 12 questions, each on a folded slip of white paper. If you can, carry several more such slips of paper on which you have written your own questions. This will help raise your stakes and maintain your interest.

In addition, carry six or more folded "green" slips of paper (non-white) in this envelope. Each of the "green" slips has a different follow-up question on it. We provide a sample list of "white" and "green" questions below that you can use to start.

Using the Kit

To use the kit in your 30-day challenge, follow these simple steps:

1. Select a white question from the envelope without looking to consciously see what it says.

2. Gather three different sets of impressions or images. Each of these is the same answer to the same question, only shown differently. Gather as much detail as you can get on these three images, to better spot the ways in which those

impressions of the answer overlap. Perhaps spend three to five minutes detailing the first image and one to two minutes on each of the others.

3. On a notepad, describe or sketch enough detail from these impressions to make it easy to see where they overlap.

4. Find the common theme(s), trends, or threads in each image.

5. Open your question and see how the common elements answer the question.

6. Add another white question to the envelope to make sure you have a minimum of six white questions in your envelope for the next time.

7. Select one of the green questions and answer it the same way. Depending upon the importance of what you're dealing with, you may want to do and use one or more green questions.

8. Replace the answered question with a new one. Always keep six or more questions in the envelope to keep the "guesser" out of the way. If you are looking for new questions and need some help, please review *Finding Problems* in Chapter 2.

You may want to keep a journal so that you can record the surprising things you start to notice, in yourself or around you, by or before the fifth consecutive day.

We suggest that you consider keeping a detailed record of your experiences, answers and observations, as would an explorer of any new, largely unexplored territory.

Remember that it is important to validate your answers before implementing any of them. See Chapter 2 for further information on the importance and means of validation.

White Questions

Here is the list of "white" questions to help you get started. As you use these up, or even before, replace them with your own questions. Part of the challenge in the "30-day challenge" is to come up with enough meaningful questions of your own!

Print these starter questions onto plain white paper, cut them up into separate slips (one question to a slip), fold the slips of paper in on themselves several times so that the written question is not immediately visible and so that the slips look more or less identical.

Here are the starter-questions:

- What main opportunity to serve should I be alert for, today?
- What can I become aware of today that will best advance me toward my goals?
- In the long run, how can I best make a positive difference in the lives of those around me?
- How can I best make sure that I keep up the practice that will best develop my abilities and well-being?
- What's another and even possibly better method than this one for discovering good answers and solutions?
- At this time, which of my illusions would it be best for me to see through to reality?
- If I am a caterpillar, what is my butterfly and how can I best get there?
- How can I best improve my material income immediately and substantially?
- What *is* the best question for me to ask now, and what is the best answer?
- At this time in my life, what have I been overlooking that could best improve my situation?
- Which one of my long-held goals is now surprisingly within my easy reach?
- What do I most need to know about this High Thinktank procedure that I'm not yet aware of?

Image-Streaming

Green Questions

Print out and cut up the following "green" questions, one question to a slip, folded in on itself. These "green" questions are follow-up questions that can be on any color paper except "white."

- How can I best make sure that I'm on the right track with this answer I've just deciphered?
- What more do I most need to know about this matter?
- What's the best concrete first step to implementing this answer or understanding?
- What's the main concern I need to watch while implementing this answer/understanding?
- What's the highest priority for my attention and action at this time?
- How can I assure the best outcomes possible for those who are affected by what I do in this context?

Closing Remarks

"Your subconscious mind never sleeps, never rests. It is always on the job." — *Joseph Murphy* [10]

In this guidebook to Image-Streaming, we have provided you with the information to learn and apply a valuable tool for releasing the inner powers of your mind.

To give you greater understanding of the process and its applications, we have described the basic principles and ideas from which the process was developed. We have taken the basic process that, by itself, is a powerful tool for building your perceptions and I.Q., and introduced you to several applications in creative problem-solving and accelerated learning.

You now have several new tools available to you that you can use to empower your own life and the lives of those around you.

One of the goals of Project Renaissance is to help provide these tools to everyone.

To expand your inventory of resources even further, there are additional tools and techniques based on Image-Streaming. There is even a procedure for developing further applications. If you wish to pursue these other resources, see Appendices D and E for further information.

If you have questions or would like to participate in further discussions, you can contact us through Project Renaissance's website, *www.winwenger.com*, or join the Yahoo listserve group at *imagestream@yahoogroups.com*.

---

[10] *The Power of Your Subconscious Mind,* Joseph Murphy (Reward Books, 2000).

Appendix A

Velvety-Smooth Breathing:
A simple way to feel better in five to ten seconds

This breathing technique provides you with a method for relaxing your mind and body to create a state that will better enable you to see your images and work with them effectively and accurately.

You've been breathing ever since you were born without having been instructed how and without paying attention to it. In other words, breathing is automatic, like your heart beat, brain wave or liver function.

But, as with your voluntary muscles, you can deliberately control your breath. By breathing deliberately in natural patterns, you can reproduce the feelings, physiology, and other conditions associated with those patterns. Your breath is a bridge of communication between your conscious intentions and your automatic responses.

Velvety-Smooth Breathing is a simple, perfectly good way to improve mental and brain performance. To feel better faster with no side effects, try *Velvety-Smooth Breathing* for one to two minutes as a start. Thereafter, use *Velvety-Smooth Breathing* at any time to feel better in five to ten seconds! Here's how:

1. Can you imagine how it would feel to be gently stroking a long smooth strip of silk or plush velvet? Imagine the sheer luxury of that feeling. For ten to thirty seconds, focus on imagining that luxurious feeling of the silk or velvet. Really get into the sheer luxury of it.

2. Now let your breathing become long, slow, and smooth. Let your breathing act as if it were stroking you, stroking you gently as you were stroking a luxurious piece of silk or plush velvet. Let your breathing stroke your whole body, head to toe, as if you were a long luxurious strip of silk or velvet.

Practice intensifying this luxurious feeling for two minutes while continuing to breathe smoothly. As you move from inhaling to exhaling and

Appendix A

back, make the transition smooth and continuous. Compare the way you feel now with the way you felt before you started *Velvety-Smooth Breathing*.

Purposefully memorize the feeling that you have achieved after your practice. Use that feeling as a takeoff point next time. On subsequent uses of *Velvety-Smooth Breathing*, you will find that you can achieve full relaxation in as little as five to ten seconds.

The occasions and situations in your life where this technique can make the biggest difference for you are exactly those when you feel least like breathing luxuriously. Any time you find yourself under stress, shoulders stiffened, or breath high in your chest, try *Velvety-Smooth Breathing*. It is at these times when you can benefit most by *Velvety-Smooth Breathing*!

Have you tried this breathing experience yet? Do so now! The two minutes invested will be paid back many times over with your improved productivity for the next two hours. Feel good now in this natural way!

Optionally, the next time you try *Velvety-Smooth Breathing*, open a container of vanilla, peppermint, or a favorite perfume. Compare how you feel while breathing this way with the feeling from *Velvety-Smooth Breathing* without such aids.

Appendix B

Self-Reporting Form

When you wish to record your experiences, create a form similar to the sample shown. You can modify the form as you see fit to meet your needs. Preferably, place the desired information on a single page, but allow yourself more space if needed for the descriptions and interpretations of your Image-Stream.

Self-Reporting Form

Title of experience: _____

Date: _____ Start time: _____ End time: _____
Time Image-Streaming began: _____ Interruptions? (Y/N): _____
( ) Listener (who?)_____ ( ) Voice recorder

Purpose: ( ) None ( ) Problem-solving ( ) Other_____
Process: ( ) *Image-Streaming* ( ) *Over-the-Wall* ( ) *Replay*
( ) Other _____
Prompting technique (if used): _____
Question or statement of problem (if applicable): _____
_____

Description of Image-Stream (continue on other pages as needed):
_____
_____
_____
_____
_____
_____

Appendix B

Linking Further Brain Areas to Consciousness	
Symbolic and/or subtle meanings	*Sensory data: 0 (none) to 10 (Wow!)*

__ Immediately apparent
__ Became apparent
__ Possible but doubtful because
    __ seemed meaningless
    __ was just beautiful
    __ was so entertaining
    __ just practicing
    __ ran out of time
__ Apparently important
 	
Describe what the image suggested as a meaning; the meaning itself; and the validation method, when available:
 	
_____
_____
_____
_____
_____
_____
_____
_____
_____
 	
Action to be taken: _____
_____
_____
	____ Images immediately, no coaxing
	____ Visual detail
	____ Clarity
	____ Color
	____ Intensity
	____ Beauty
	____ In 3-D
	____ Saw movement
	____ Hearing
	____ Taste
	____ Smell
	____ Texture/touch
	____ Movement/feel
	____ Pressure/feel
	____ Warm/cool
	____ Emotional/atmospheric feel
	____ A knowing or knowingness
	____ Exultation or other special feeling
	____ Other senses/perceptions:
	    (*describe*)
	
	_____
	_____
	_____
	_____
	_____
	_____
	_____
	_____
	_____
	_____
	_____

Appendix C
Prompting Techniques

In Chapter 1, we referred to prompting techniques to assist you in obtaining images if you were having difficulty in starting your Image-Stream. We included an example of one technique for use with a partner. We provide you here with 22 additional prompting techniques. Refer back to Chapter 1 for instructions on when and how to use these techniques.

1. **After-Image** is another way to get inner visual impressions going. Stare at a small light (not the sun!—20 to 40 watts only) for half a minute. After staring at the light, you should have momentary after-images when you close your eyes. These are left-over prints of that light on the retina at the back of your eye. You may see a blob of light or color, perhaps a line or so. Describe what you see in detail and continue describing it as that after-image changes color and shape.

After-images that are not reinforced last only a few seconds. If you reinforce your after-images through attention and description, they can last for minutes. We've even found that some after-images can last for up to 4 hours! If yours fades out after a few moments, recharge it with the light again and resume describing.

At some point during the process of examining and describing your after-images, you may notice other images, whether just trace impressions or momentary pictures.

It's these other images that we are aiming to reach and describe in this experience. So please notice when a new image appears, and switch to describing that new image in the present tense, as if you were still looking at it, even if it was only a momentary glimpse that you caught. With sufficiently forceful, detailed, and sustained flow of description, more images will come.

Appendix C

2. **Worth describing** — you may have been getting blobs of color, lines, patterns, or other visual impressions and not reported them because you thought they were too trivial to mention. Or, you may have been getting impressions in other sensory channels — sounds, odors, or feelings of pressure or movement. All of these impressions are inner phenomena worth reporting. If you describe them in a rapid, detailed, and sustained flow, you will find they will lead to other impressions, some of which clearly will not seem so trivial to you.

If, after 10-20 minutes, this flow has not led to any other kind of imagery, continue with your eyes closed and:
- Deliberately look beyond the color as if beyond a colored screen, just a few feet further, and see..... Whatever impression, resume describing from there.
- Or, breathe as if to "breathe in" the nearest of the colors, clearing the way to see other impressions.....

3. **Phosphenes** — gently rub your own closed eyes like a sleepy child, and describe the resulting light and color patterns. Continue describing what is there....

The next two procedures can become so introspective that it's easy to nod off. So for these two procedures, we recommend using a listener to identify the attention cues as described in the *Helper Technique*, page 18.

4. **Stream from memory** —Recall a real scene (a very beautiful landscape or object, for instance), a past dream, or an invented beautiful garden or park. Even if these are just made-up story words at first and not a perceived experience, begin describing the scene in as rich detail as possible. The Image-Streamer is like a reporter, sending that description to the Listener from

Image-Streaming

within the scene as if it were going on right now instead of being a memory. While you are describing this memory, the Listener watches your closed eyes closely. The Listener, seeing them move under the lids, seizes that occasion to ask, "What did you see just then?"..... It's noticing these images that is our key and what the Image-Streamer should pursue, whether they are memories or new fresh images. This is especially relevant when images appear that don't fit the "story" or scene being described.

Keep encouraging the description until it is flowing, even if it has to begin from word-memories or make-believe and not pictures, until images are in fact flowing. Once description is flowing, the Listener gets out of the way. Do not interrupt with questions. Do not provide any more encouragement than a slight "um-hmm." The flow of description will bring a flow of pictures if the description is in richly textured detail, sustained without interruption.

---

5. **Door** — similar to *Stream from Memory*, except instead of a garden, park, or remembered beautiful scene, you as the Image-Streamer picture being in front of a closed door. Describe the door and the feel of the door as if you had just placed a hand on it. Then, suddenly fling open the door to catch by surprise whatever's there to see on the other side of it. The Listener should ask for your first impressions of what was there or what might have been there, getting you to describe that impression, even if it was barely there, as if it were still present. See what else comes into view.

If nothing at all came, repeat the door procedure but with colorful, textured window curtains, or jump over a high wall. Maintain the idea that something unexpected but valuable or useful will likely be in view on the other side if you open the view suddenly. The more unexpected the contents of the imagery, the better your chances that the image is coming from deeper within your brain and not just from the conscious

Appendix C

treadmill portion (which is likely to deal up pictures of what you already consciously know about the context or present situation). The more surprising the imagery contents, the better your chances of getting sensitive, comprehensive, and fresh perceptions and insights.

---

6. **Music** — Listen to some richly textured music with your eyes closed and your recorder ready to record. Preferably, use classical music, French Impressionist music, or progressive jazz, with enough variation in content to attract and involve your more sensitive inner resources. Notice when you have an image and begin describing it. Persist in your description. Remember Walt Disney's *Fantasia*? A Listener would be invaluable at this point to spot your attention cues when some strong image starts to catch your attention.

---

7. **Background sounds** — Pick up a recording of background sounds and listen to them with your eyes closed. Describe in detail the images that these sounds evoke for you, even if the description is not what the sounds appear to be logically. If possible, use a Listener who can be your spotter, alerting you when you exhibit an attention cue. The Listener should ask, "What were you seeing just then?" When the sounds end, keep on describing. Take notice when other images emerge and describe them in turn. This moves you from the guided imagery brought on by the music to the undirected form—Image-Streaming.

---

8. **House blindfolded** — Go around your house blindfolded, feeling different objects. Describe at length the appearance of each item you feel. Or, get someone to set up a grab bag for you of many highly diverse objects. Then, feel each object and describe the feeling of the object regardless of whether you can identify it. Describe the size, the shape, the texture, and the consistency. Is there an odor or sound associated with the

Image-Streaming

object? See if at some point with your eyes closed, you don't notice other images also coming..... Trying to discover these characteristics puts your system in the market for *more perceptions* with some of those *perceptions* being the images you are seeking

---

9. **Air sculpting** — With your eyes closed, begin sculpting some object in thin air or use imaginary clay. Hold the sculpture in your hands and describe its appearance in detail. See if other images begin to emerge for you.

---

10. **Passenger** — When riding as a passenger in a train, bus, or car, describe in detail with your eyes kept closed what you think is the appearance of the landscape or street scenes you are riding through. See if other images begin to emerge for you.

Each of these scenarios calls upon other resources to help you visualize your way through their situations. How many times have you had to feel your way through the dark to some goal, even in your own house, such as going to the bathroom during the night? Remember those stories about being kidnapped and the victim figuring out where he was while blindfolded in the escape car?

---

11. **Eat blindfolded** — describe the appearance, in detail, of what you're eating. Include all of your senses. Describe the texture of the food, its flavor, its odor, and more. See if other images begin to emerge for you.

Arrange four to five different aromas from your spice rack. Set them before you. Shuffle them around with eyes closed and try to identify each one. See if any of the aromas trigger further visual images. If they trigger only memories instead, describe a scene from

Appendix C

one of those memories as vividly and in detail as you can and see if other images develop which can then also be described....

---

12. **At night with all lights off** while inside your bathroom with your eyes open, orient toward the lights, turn them on, and immediately close eyes! You should find some rather elaborate after-images or even a scene of some sort. Describe in detail and see what else comes.....

Variant: Flick the bathroom lights on and off rapidly several times with eyes closed and proceed as above. Describe your after-images with the lights finally turned on or off.

---

13. Obtain a simple **stroboscope** if you are not epileptic. Set the stroboscopic light to somewhere between 4 and 12 beats per second. Look into that stroboscopic light with eyes kept closed and describe the evoked colors and patterns for awhile, staying alert to other images.

If no other kind of image happens after 10-15 minutes of this, start describing some imagined or remembered scene in detail, while continuing to look into the strobe light with closed eyes and be alert to such imagery as may develop for you. If nothing additional still comes, try again with the strobe set to different frequencies. Choose one that makes the greatest color and pattern displays to your closed eyes.

---

14. **Read a good, fully entertaining novel** or story long enough to really get into it. Then, with a recorder set up, *word-paint* some scenes from the story, going beyond those described by the author. See what else unfolds. Or remember a favorite story and do the same with that story. See if you can detect other images happening as you get well into the rapid descriptive

Image-Streaming

flow. If so, then move from directed to undirected free-association imagery.

The key is to get anything at all started from which to describe as rapidly as possible so that you have to reach beyond your conscious thoughts, so that you force your conscious mind to accept fresh input from your subtler resources.

You can make work of this activity, or you can treat each of these options as fresh, enjoyable new explorations, bringing you new experiences and opening new skills. Because we perceive more with pleasure, we suggest that if you need any of these prompting procedures, make them as enjoyable an exploration as you can. To do so improves the chances that your senses and your mind will open to new perceptions.

The following eight procedures are favorites for many people. Each provides a special guided imagery device that may open into some enjoyable unguided free-flow Image-Streams. Even if you are already able to start your Image-Stream without a prompting process, you may want to occasionally vary your entry into your Image-Streaming with one of the following guided starts.

15. **Tree and cloud**—Imagine and describe yourself walking in a meadow. Find yourself going uphill in this meadow toward a single immense tree at the very top of the hill. Engage all your senses in the experience. Describe the warm breeze, the sunshine on your neck, the colors and smells of the wild flowers, the pull of walking up a gradual slope for a long time, the sounds of the grasses, the sounds of your own steps in those grasses, and of your breathing. To rest from climbing that long hill, lie down in the soft moss at the base of the tree. Look up the tree's immense trunk, between its branches low and high, near and far, at the sky. See the clouds moving across the sky, as you look at them from between the branches. Does the movement of the clouds make you feel like the tree is moving

Appendix C

instead? Experience how the movement of the clouds across the sky makes you feel as if it's the tree, the hill and you who are moving instead of the clouds. Let that movement take you wherever it will, describing as you go.....

16. **Wind-blown leaf** — Be a leaf, or the fluff of a dandelion, moving with the wind, around corners of buildings and over trees and swiftly racing across an immense landscape.... Describe as you go, toward wherever the wind carries you....

17. **Beneath the boat** — Imagine gently riding a boat on a lake or downstream in a broad, slow river. Peer down into the water, past the shimmering surface and the ripples. Try to see what's below there. At first, perhaps you see only the reflection of light from the water or the ripples and sparkle in this imaginary boat ride. But, as you peer more intently, you begin to see.....

18. **Climbing a steep hillside or mountainside, through a forest** — describe this fully multi-sensory experience. As you approach the top, you near a clearing, the scenery unexpectedly opens up to show you .... What?

People who are oriented toward science and technology often like the following three prompting procedures.

19. **The elevator you are riding in stops; its door is opening — where?** Is this some scene or place that you've not seen before? Quickly describe your very first impression!

20. **Be a seed or spore** that has been floating comfortably in outer space for millions of years. Now approach some world that is

Image-Streaming

different from any world that you've ever seen. Drift down onto that world, reporting back as you go, rapidly describing in detail as you see and experience more and more of this new world ....

Now be a person on that world. Suddenly look down where your feet would be if you were human—what do you see? What surface are you on? Continue describing...

---

21. **Radio pulse** — imagine what it might be like to simply flow as a pulse of electricity along a wire into a powerful radio transmitter directed into outer space. What would it be like to be a radio wave traveling across space, between stars, between galaxies, to..... ? Quickly describe your first impression...

This last device frequently gives rise to truly great, illuminating experiences....

22. **A tremendous light** is sensed on the other side of a door, at the head of a long staircase. A sense of excitement and expectation seems to await you on the far side of that door. Describe the door. Feel it, stroke it, and describe it further. You sense something very bright or powerful behind it. Suddenly, open the door and rise exhilarated into that light! There is so much light that you can't quite see what's there, but you begin to clear the air by breathing in the light. You breathe slowly and luxuriously, feeling more exhilarated with each breath of light you take in. And, there you begin to see around you.....

Appendix D
Project Renaissance Methods and Processes

Listed below are the methods and processes developed in association with Project Renaissance over the years. The list is fairly comprehensive but continues to grow. See also Appendix E for a list of sources for further information on the methods and processes presented in this Core Book and listed below.

In this Core Book:
- Image-Streaming
- Image-Streaming for Creative Problem Solving
- Image-Streaming for Children
- Image-Streaming for Groups
- Co-Tripping
- What Did I Leave Out
- Writer's Block (Fiction and Non-fiction)
- Over-the-Wall
- Instant Replay
- World Next Door
- Dream Interpretation
- Velvety-Smooth Breathing
- Predictive Imagery
- High Thinktank
- Cognitive Structural Enhancement

From other resources:
- Portable Memory Bank—A simple technique to reinforce your perceptions and creativity.
- Freenoting — A writing brainstorm in some context can bring up a wealth of insights you didn't think you knew.
- Walk in the Woods

Image-Streaming

- Crabapple
- Win-Win Finder — Incentive Equilibrium analysis finds solutions so both sides win.
- Borrowed Genius — How to build skills by borrowing from a true genius.
- Flick-Gazing
- Sidebands by sudden capture
- Sidebands by flash awareness
- Evoked Sidebands
- Sidebands by visual fixation
- Gravel Gulch — An easy 4-step procedure of stretching to see further possibilities.
- Integrating Knowledge
- Dynamic Format — Simple procedures for running better, more productive meetings, groups, clubs and classes.
- Toolbuilder — Using your best problem-solving methods to find even better methods.
- Beachhead — Visualizing the future to bring back innovations as yet not dreamed of today.
- Idea Generator
- STARS — Spaced Tape and Replay System
- TAVIT — Tape and Visual Technique
- Windtunnel—Creative problem-solving technique that quickly blows through that familiar phase and digs for fresh insights.
- DIDA –Determine, Intend, Detail, and After
- The Game of Gotcha
- Noise-Removal Breathing
- Relief-Breathing
- Mirror-Breathing
- Calm-Breathing
- Three Doors
- Artist's Eyes

Appendix E
Resources and References for Further Support

Selected Books by Win Wenger
- *Discovering the Obvious*
- *Beyond Teaching and Learning*
- *How to Increase Your Intelligence*
- *How to Be a Better Teacher, Today*
- *A Method for Personal Growth and Development*
- *The Einstein Factor* (with Richard Poe)
- *Beyond OK*

Core Books
- *Win Wenger's Image-Streaming* by Charles Roman
- *Win Wenger's Super Skills for Students: The top techniques for Socratic learning* by Isa McKechnie
- *Win Wenger's Dynamic Teaching* by Harman Benda
- *End Writer's Block Forever* by Mark Bossert
- *Breathing As a Way of Life* by Win Wenger
- *Borrowed Genius* by Win Wenger
- *Evoked Sidebands* by Win Wenger
- *Workbook for PS43* by Win Wenger

and others to come…

Audio Programs
- *Brain Boosters—20 Minutes a Day to a More Powerful Intelligence* by Win Wenger (Nightingale-Conant)
- *The Einstein Factor* by Win Wenger and Richard Poe (Nightingale-Conant)
- *The Genius Code* by Win Wenger and Paul Scheele (Learning Strategies Corp.

Image-Streaming

Training Courses
- The Beyond-Einstein Training Intensive
- Invention and Discovery Training
- Visual Thinking – The One-Day Core Training
- In-house Faculty Training for Teachers:
    - —Teach Smarter, Not Harder
    - —Become a Socrateur for Fun and Profit
    - —Beyond Teaching and Learning
- The One-Week Renaissance in Art or Music
- Toward a General Theory of Systems
- The Dynamics of Civilization
- Rebuild the Very Foundations of Understanding
- Psychegenic Methodology

Web-Based Resources
- Highly interactive and one of the most popular Internet listgroups today — *imagestream@yahoogroups.com*

- Official website of Project Renaissance, *www.winwenger.com* — a great resource for past and current information on the processes and methods developed by Project Renaissance. It is continually expanded and updated, with new information, techniques, news, and the *Winsights* column.

- Membership newsletter, *The Stream*, sent by email.

Books Online
- *On Incentives as a Preferred Instrument of Corporate and Public Policy* — a plethora of incentive proposals, ingenious solutions to thorny problems, and techniques for creating new solutions.

Appendix E

- *You Are Brighter Than You Think!* — Combining Socratic method with Einstein's "deep-thought" technique promotes human intellect to function at its finest.

- *Two Guaranteed Ways to Profoundly Improve Your Intelligence* — Held-breath underwater swimming and Image-Streaming as powerful agents of greater effectiveness.

- Chapter 1 of *Beyond Teaching and Learning* — The full text of Chapter 1 of this book, with many hot tips for accelerated learning and increased understanding, and for accessing and retrieving your unconsciously held awarenesses. Learn like a genius!

- *The Philosopher's Stone* — For children, a fantasy tale of courage and wisdom. Illustrated, with an addendum for parents.

- *Dew Song* — For children, a gentle tale of beauty and fantasy that could hold real-world truths. Illustrated.

Conferences:
- The annual *Double Festival* held in the Baltimore/Washington D.C. Area — A leading seminar in the fields of creative problem-solving and accelerated learning.

- The annual *Spring Workshop* for Project Renaissance trainers and new students, alternating between London, England, and the Baltimore/Washington area.

- *Invention-on-Demand Training Workshop* in the Fall in the Maryland/Washington D.C. area.

www.ingramcontent.com/pod-product-compliance
Lightning Source LLC
LaVergne TN
LVHW090945240325
806685LV00011B/305